Look to the Hills

THE JEWISH PUBLICATION SOCIETY
Philadelphia • Jerusalem   *5756-1995*

...Look to the Hills

Hazel Krantz

Copyright © 1995 by Hazel Krantz
Cover illustration copyright © 1995 by Richard Martin
First edition   All rights reserved
Manufactured in the United States of America

Krantz, Hazel.
  Look to the hills
    p.   cm.
  Summary: Growing up in Colorado in the 1880s and
1890s, Sally finds that her Jewish faith has a significant effect
on her social standing and her life in general.
ISBN 0-8276-0552-8 (cloth)
ISBN 0-8276-0571-4 (paper)
  1. Jews—United States—Juvenile fiction. [1. Jews—United
States—Fiction.   2. Frontier and pioneer life—
Colorado-Fiction.   3. Colorado—Fiction.]   I. Title
PZ7.K8594Lo   1955
[Fic]—dc20   95-16732
                                                    CIP
                                                     AC

No part of this publication may be reproduced or transmitted
in any form or by any means, electronic or mechanical,
including photocopy, recording, or any information storage
or retrieval system, except for brief passages in connection
with a critical review, without permission in writing from the
publisher:
The Jewish Publication Society
1930 Chestnut Street
Philadelphia, PA 19103

This book is for Kerry

Contents

Acknowledgments

Many thanks to my literary agent, Joseph Rhodes, for his fine assistance. Thank you to my editor, Bruce Black, for his confidence and excellent suggestions Most of all, thanks to the "first reader," Michael Krantz.

I wish to make special mention of one of my resource books without which this story could not have been written: *Pioneers, Peddlers, and Tsadikim*, by Ida Uchill. I am grateful to Ida Uchill, not only for her excellent book, but also for her friendship and encouragement.

Hazel Krantz
Fort Collins, Colorado

Fact or Fiction?

This is a work of fiction. Sometimes novels contain a statement: "This is a work of fiction. Any resemblance between the characters in the story and real people is coincidental."

That is not true of this story. Some of the characters are fictional, but many are based on real individuals. Most of the events are fictional, but, then again, some of them really happened. I have made three lists, one for fictional people based on real individuals, one for fictional people created for the story, and another for actual, non-fictional people who lived at the time, so you will be able to tell them apart.

Characters Based on Real People

Dr. Sigmund Gottesman—The character of Dr. Gottesman is modeled on Dr. John Elsner, an early Jewish physician in Denver.

Daniel Rabinowitz—Daniel, although a fictional character, represents the doctors who so tirelessly cared for the patients at the National Jewish Hospital, particularly a much-beloved physician, Dr. Charles Spivak, also an immigrant from Russia. Today, Dr. Spivak's descendants, including young Jacob and Benjamin Spivak and their grandmother, Sally, live in Denver and Fort Collins.

The members of the confirmation class—The clothing worn by the people in the confirmation class was suggested by a photo of the Class of 1887, Temple Emanuel's first confirmation class.

Characters Created for the Story

Sally Gottesman
Carrie
Ingrid
Lars
Nat and *Lillie Wald*
Gottesman Family (other than Dr. Gottesman)
Elvira Gottlieb
Miss Griswold and *Miss West*
Nursery school children and elementary school children
Mrs. Howe
Other Fort Collins people

xiii • *Fact or Fiction?*

Non-fictional Characters

Frances Jacobs—Although the incidents in the story are fictional, they are typical of Mrs. Jacobs' activities. The story about the two girls who took an overdose of morphine is true, taken from a newspaper account of the time. The account of Mrs. Jacobs' funeral and the honor bestowed on her by her selection to be depicted on the state capitol dome are true.

Abraham Jacobs—Respected businessman and pioneer, Abraham Jacobs helped draft the Colorado State Constitution. Husband of Frances Jacobs.

Evelyn and Benjamin Jacobs—Children of Frances and Abraham Jacobs. Evelyn was a teacher, and then principal of the 29th Street Primary School. Benjamin was an attorney.

Rabbi William S. Friedman—Rabbi Friedman served Temple Emanuel of Denver from 1889 until 1938. He not only strengthened his congregation, but also worked for the welfare of the entire city. One of his chief interests was the National Jewish Hospital.

Rabbi Mendes de Sola—Rabbi Friedman's predecessor, de Sola became an agnostic after retiring from the rabbinate and wrote several books on the subject.

xiv • *Fact or Fiction?*

Otto Mears—The famous Pathfinder of the San Juans, who daringly built roads through the mountains, was a good friend of Frances Jacobs and was instrumental in having her portrait placed in the state capitol dome. He was also a friend of Chief Ouray of the Ute tribe, and it is said that he spoke the Ute language with a Yiddish accent.

Wolfe Londoner—Merchant and mayor of Denver, 1889–1891.

Eugene Field—Editor of the *Tribune* and poet, an irrepressible prankster.

Look to the Hills

வ்வ்வ் *Chapter 1*

"It's in the Bible," Sally Gottesman reminded her friend Carrie. "'And Ahasuerus, the king, commanded his wife Vashti to come before him with her royal crown, to show the people and princes her beauty. And Vashti refused to come.' I'm going to be Vashti. I think she's been entirely too neglected."

"You're not serious, are you?" giggled Carrie Rosenthal. "In the temple?"

Sally shifted her load of school books—Latin, English, Mathematics—twirled her long gray skirt and took another careful step down the front steps of Denver High School, an imposing brick building, three stories high, with two pointed towers decorated with scrolled stonework. "If Vashti had been an obedient wife, there would not have been a Queen Esther. And then," she pressed her hand to her mouth in mock despair, "what would have happened to our ancestors? Hung by Haman, every one!"

Laughing, Carrie held on to the stair railing. "You sound just like Rabbi de Sola."

"Shh," said Sally in mock horror. "We cannot offend the rabbi. After all the trouble with the last one. At least, not until after confirmation."

"I don't know why I wore my good kid boots." Carrie stepped gingerly onto the soggy sidewalk. It was March, 1886, and the weather was normal for Denver. On Monday there had been a blizzard with swirling winds and the heavy wet snow of early spring. Today the temperature had hit sixty degrees, and the snow rushed to melt, moisture spiraling upward into the dry Colorado air.

An open buggy passed, spraying mud from the unpaved street. Hastily, the girls jumped away, protecting their skirts. Dave Ginsburg and Joseph Weinberg sauntered by, horsing around with their books. Dave gave Joe a push and, with a loud wail, Joe landed in the snow, "accidently" spewing the girls with gobs of snow. As they squealed in alarm, Dave bowed and apologized. "Oh, sorry. So sorry." And he kicked more snow on them as Joe scrambled, snickering, to his feet.

Noses in the air, the girls proceeded toward the corner. "Yes, and, as we were saying, our dear rabbi is right. Our confirmation class of 1886 represents the flowering of modern Jewry, the finest examples of American youth," declared Sally. The elderly rabbi did sometimes say that, trying to get on the good side of his unruly class.

"Pardon me while I throw up," said Carrie loudly.

Sally looked at her disapprovingly. "How indelicate!"

A couple of snowballs struck them from behind.

Yelling, the girls ran as fast as their long skirts would let them, to the corner and the horsecar stop. Sally straightened her flat schoolgirl hat and attempted to tuck in her reddish blonde hair, escaping in every direction no matter how many hairpins she anchored it with. She was tall, with dark blue eyes that tended to look at you very directly, a clear straight forehead, and delicately blonde eyebrows. Her nose, to her despair, was slightly hooked; the fact that she had inherited it from Grandfather Isaac Gottesman back in Germany did not comfort her.

Carrie was smaller—daintier, as Sally would describe her. She had a creamy complexion and large, widely-spaced brown eyes, usually full of innocent wonder, betrayed by a saucy quirk at the corners of her full mouth. She drew her cape closer around her as a gust of wind swirled up Colfax Avenue. "Want to come to my house?"

"Not this afternoon," said Sally. "I'm going downtown to Uncle Abraham Jacobs' store to buy the fabric for my costume."

Carrie's eyes widened with excitement and she wiggled enticingly, humming a Arabian dancing girl melody. "And in this corner, Vashti, the scorned queen. Because she did the hoochy-koochy dance."

"Don't laugh," said Sally. "This is a serious matter. Vashti was a wronged woman. What right did Ahasuerus have to tell her to come to his throne room? Maybe she had something better to do."

Carrie went hoochy-koochying down Colfax Avenue as the omnibus run by the Denver Transfer Company, a splendid cream-colored vehicle decorated with a fancy medallion and drawn by two prancing horses, came down the street. The driver reined his steeds to a halt and Sally climbed in, paid her fare and sat, cupping her chin in her hand, gazing out the window.

She found the city endlessly fascinating. It was always changing, in a frenzy of building. Only twenty-six years old, if you didn't count the little log settlement that existed beside Cherry Creek before the big gold rush of 1859, the city now boasted substantial brick homes, bristling with bay windows and fancy turrets and surrounded by elaborately worked wrought iron fences. She gazed at the home of dapper Wolfe Londoner, all trimmed in white stone, with a turret and dormer topped by lacy ironwork, and the huge Tabor mansion where Augusta Tabor lived alone since her millionaire husband deserted her for showgirl Baby Doe . . .

Denver's juiciest scandal.

As the horses turned into Larimer Street, Sally saw the new Chever Building, a square edifice three stories high with fancy trim around the top, housing the Exchange Bank. Then the horses passed the elegant Tabor Opera House, the Wonderland Theater, the Palace Theater, Salomon's Dry Goods Store, and Joslin's Department Store. In the distance Sally could see Denver University and, at the outskirts of town, the giant smelter, melting down the products of Colorado's mines—silver and gold—and sending into the air a haze of smoke, veiling the mountains in the west.

The horses went clipping along, their hooves splattering through the mud, surrounded by a throng of horses pulling other vehicles. There were wagons piled with merchandise and ore from the mines, elegant open buggies, smart pony carts, family carriages, and people on horseback. Pedestrians dodged the traffic, ladies with bobbing bustles picking their way through the mire, shawled women trailing children, boys in knickers (with the pants fitted snugly just below the knee) darting around the horses, bewhiskered miners in town for a spree, and cowboys from the cattle ranges, wearing wide-brimmed stained hats and muddy boots and lurching along, somewhat unsteady out of the saddle and rocked by strong drinks offered in Denver's many saloons. Drifting through the open windows of the horsecar were the odors of the city, the acrid fumes from the smelters, the smell of horse manure, and, beneath it all, the sweet shy beginnings of growing things.

The horsecar stopped near Abraham Jacobs' O.K. Store and Sally got out. Entering the shop, blinking a little at the dimness, she found Uncle Abraham bent over a ledger, frowning as he studied its contents, with lines of worry creasing his face. He was not her real uncle, but the Jacobs family and the Gottesmans had been close friends ever since Abraham and Frances Jacobs had moved to Denver from Central City.

Sally was about to tiptoe to the back of the store where Ida, the clerk, was busily arranging women's hats, when Abraham saw her.

His round face broke into a smile. "Sally, little one. Come here."

"I don't want to disturb you, Uncle Abraham. Ida can help me. I'm looking for material for a costume. For the Purim Ball."

"And you think I will let anyone else choose the right goods for your costume? For the most beautiful Queen Esther in Denver?"

Sally swallowed, and said nothing. If he wanted to think she would be Queen Esther, that was his right.

"Anyway," he admitted, as they walked toward the fabrics corner. "It's good to get away from bad news for a while." He sighed.

"Hard times, Uncle Abraham?"

He shrugged. "I can't complain. After all, I've

had my ups and downs before." Abraham still spoke with a trace of a German accent.

But Sally knew that the O.K. Store wasn't doing well. One of the earliest pioneers in Colorado, Abraham Jacobs had helped write its Constitution. Well known for his absolute integrity, he had been one of the people entrusted with setting the price of an ounce of gold. Until the railroads came in, he'd owned the stage that went to southern Colorado and Santa Fe. President of B'nai B'rith, a prominent member of the Masonic Order, he was one of the Coloradoans selected to welcome President Grant when he visited Denver in 1880. But a fire in his Central City store had cost him $50,000, an enormous fortune in those days. Abraham came to Denver and was trying to succeed with this small store, but it could not compete with large establishments like Salomon's, Appel's and Joslin's.

He unrolled a bolt of white chiffon.

"Um, Uncle Abraham . . . I was thinking of red. Red net."

"Red? But Esther always wears white."

Sally shrugged. "Where is it written . . . ?"

He laughed. "Red it is. Now for the royal jewels."

There were spangles and silver cloth and shiny buttons imitating diamonds.

"Oh, I shall be regal. A savage queen," said Sally.

Abraham wagged his finger at her. "Esther was a nice Jewish girl. Even when a queen she remembered her family."

"Yes, but she was very, very rich. The Ahasuerus family owned the whole country."

"Well, I guess Rabbi de Sola is teaching you well. You know your history. And so, you are to be confirmed this Shavuot?"

"June second. We're to have a party. You and Aunt Frank are invited of course."

"If not, I would break down the door." He was laughing. It made Sally feel better to see Uncle Abraham more cheerful.

"And what's new with Aunt Frank?"

"What isn't new? She's running to the poor people in the tent city. She's helping the, er, bad girls."

"Whores," Sally said helpfully.

Abraham looked only mildly shocked. He knew Sally.

"Well, she says no one else cares for them.

"And she's all excited about that new kindergarten idea she heard about in San Francisco. They're putting one in over on West Colfax, for the children of poor mothers who have to work.

"Not to mention her concern for the lungers. She's always stopping them on the street and asking them if they're taken care of. They're not, of course. It's the poor people who get tuberculosis working in the sweat shops of New York. Someone tells them to go to Denver for the good air. So they spend their last cent on a railroad ticket. It doesn't occur to them that people have to eat in Colorado too. Most of them can't speak English and they're too sick to work."

"She can't take care of the whole world," Sally exclaimed. "She'll get sick."

Abraham opened his hands in defeat. "That's my Frankie. I think it's good for her. She forgets the fire . . . and the boy. . . ."

His voice trailed off. Sally remembered the loss of one of their three children just before they came to Denver. "How are Evelyn and Benjamin?" she asked quickly.

"Good," he said, cheered by the thoughts of his living children. "Evelyn is teaching already, first grade. And Ben's to be a lawyer soon. And your brothers?"

"Simon's at the School of Mines in Golden and Ephraim is in Boulder at the University of Colorado."

Abraham nodded approvingly. "When we formed the state, the first thing we said was . . . education. All at once, we started colleges. Do you know where a community gets its prosperity?"

Sally fidgeted. Uncle Abraham sounded as if he were about to give one of his speeches. She wanted to go home and start on the costume. "No," she mumbled.

He raised a finger. "Education!" he intoned. "With an educated population you have efficient industry. And that brings prosperity."

Sally put an agreeable smile on her face and moved firmly toward the cash register. Uncle

Abraham quoted her an absurd price, far below the value of the merchandise. While he was wrapping the fabric in brown paper and as Sally was fishing into her purse for the money, the door of the store creaked open.

As Frances Jacobs came storming in, Abraham put the bundle down on the counter with a thump. "Frances, what's happened to you? You look as if you've been in a tornado."

"It was the most terrible thing, Abraham. Hello, Sally. Maybe this is not for your ears." Nervously she adjusted her hat, which had come all askew. "Well, I guess it's all right. You're almost sixteen and it's time you knew the ways of the world."

Sally refrained from replying that with two older brothers, she already knew the ways of the world.

Frances opened her purse, took out a handkerchief, and wiped her face. A strong whiff of the Grandpa's Tar Soap she always carried—for she believed that the hungry were often unwashed—filled the air. Involuntarily, Sally made a face.

Frances leaned back, mopping her face in a vigorous, not quite ladylike manner. The Jacobs' family was in the Social Register, accepted into the most exclusive society in Denver, but Frances didn't seem to give a hoot about that. Not a pretty woman, she had what was known as an "interesting" face, with blunt strong features and dark hair drawn back severely in a bun, revealing unpretty prominent ears. "Abraham calls them my

13 • *Chapter One*
listening ears," she was known to say, laughing at herself. She was dressed in simple unadorned clothing, a dark suit and a plain white blouse, her only ornament a gold pin at the throat. Her hat did not trail fashionable ostrich feathers and artificial flowers but was round and plain, trimmed with a navy ribbon. Her high-buttoned shoes, with the tiniest of "baby Louis" high heels, were made for walking rather than fashion.

Abraham faced her eagerly. It was clear that, despite her lack of glamor, he adored his wife. Sally felt a pang, the way she did sometimes on a autumn day when the aspen leaves shimmered in perfect gold. Somehow, although she was only fifteen, she knew the love and respect the Jacobses had for one another was a rare thing.

"So tell us," said Abraham.

"Suicide! Oh, most dreadful."

"Who," cried Abraham. "Anyone we know?"

"Oh, no, no. At least you don't know them. I was down on Market Street . . ."

Sally clutched her parcel, her eyes wide. Market Street was where the "bad" girls Abraham talked about plied their trade. She was forbidden under any circumstances to go there. And here Aunt Frank mentioned it as if it were the most natural thing in the world! She was so much more interesting than other adults.

"I don't like your going there." Abraham shook his head.

"I know, darling, but there was this girl Anna,

and I knew she had a terrible fever. Those girls are so neglected. I brought her some medicine. After all, Abraham, everyone acts as if these people were some kind of untouchable tribe. They're our girls . . ."

"Not Jewish girls," said Abraham severely.

"No, of course not," she replied absently. "Although how do you know? Some of the Jews coming into West Colfax are pretty desperate. These are mostly farm girls, children of home-steaders, lost in the city. Some of them come from the poor families down by the river. Anyway . . ."

"The suicide," Abraham prompted.

"There were two girls living down the hall from Anna who attempted suicide. Your father, Sally—an angel, a medical angel—came when I called him and saved them. They had taken morphine."

She caught her breath and fanned herself with the soggy handkerchief. "According to witnesses, the two girls, Effie and Allie, had been drinking heavily. They were seen at Christian's saloon around noon, drinking whiskey. Then they went to Lyneman's drug store, where Effie bought a dram of morphine. The clerk took her to be a morphine fiend and gave it to her. Don't you think drug stores should be forbidden to supply mor-phine to dope fiends, Abraham?"

"I do," he nodded.

"Then the girls went back to where they lived." Frances glanced uneasily at Sally. "Er . . . Mattie

Silk's boarding house."

"Bordello," muttered Sally.

In spite of her distress, Frances grinned. A twitch of amusement appeared at the corners of Abraham's mouth.

"Well, apparently the girls went up to Effie Pryor's room in a drunken state and they decided to have a suicide pact. Someone heard Effie say, 'Allie, you are not game,' and then Allie said 'See if I'm not.' No one thought anything of it until one of Effie's friends came around and knocked on the door and didn't get an answer. She asked Nels Christian to raise her up to the transom and she looked in. She gave one shriek and collapsed in Nels' arms." Frances paused dramatically.

Sally just stared at her, open-mouthed.

"So," said Abraham.

"Well, naturally, they broke down the door and found the two girls in bed, nearly dead. Their faces were black and distorted. I heard the screams and ran in from where I was taking care of Anna. It was horrible.

"I sent for Dr. Gottesman and the police surgeon came and together they brought the girls around. I'm still shaking."

"I don't want you to go to that place," Abraham said firmly.

"But don't you see, dear? That's where I'm need-ed. Those girls live such sordid lives."

They were still arguing as Sally left the store and headed for the horsecar stop. Somehow, she felt transported to Market Street where girls probably not much older than herself were so miserable they overdosed on whiskey and morphine. It was such a sad, sad feeling. Like the lungers hemorrhaging on the street.

The world had so much misery.

But it was spring and it was almost time for Purim.

She climbed onto the horsecar, thinking about the ball and the sensation she'd make when she arrived in her costume . . .Vashti, the woman who dared talk back to Ahasuerus!

wwww Chapter 2

Dr. Sigmund Gottesman, Sally's father, had built his home on the outskirts of the city, where the air was clean and there was a field where his horses could run free. He had seen enough of lung disease, which he felt was caused by poverty, improper food, and above all, poor ventilation. He wanted his family, which extended to his animals, to have space.

Sally left the horsecar at its last stop and walked sedately down the new sidewalk under bare-branched young elms, toward the house. That is, she tried to move in a sedate, ladylike fashion, but her feet kept skipping as if she were six years old.

She hugged the parcel, rehearsing in her mind the shocked surprise that would greet her costume. She had it all figured out. There would be bloomers, like the ones Amelia Bloomer had invented. Scandalous, scandalous, ten years ago! Women in pants! It was forbidden in the Bible, in the Torah itself. But now, although frowned upon, there were times when women did wear pants, knickers, or divided skirts so they wouldn't have to ride horseback sidesaddle. Colorado women were not given to riding sidesaddle.

Yes, there would be bloomers—harem pants, very Oriental, of the red net material, with discreet stockings underneath, of course. And Sally gyrated slightly in one of Carrie's hoochy-koochys. A severe-looking man driving by in a carriage gave her a disapproving look. The cloth of silver around her waist, maybe dangling with a long tassel. More of the same around her head, low on the forehead.

No corset. Vashti would never wear a corset. Balancing her books and the package, she felt around her waist. Pretty slender. Although not as slim as some. The Gottesmans tended to be big-boned, another gift from the mysterious Grandfather Isaac in Germany. Also big breasted . . . from the equally mysterious Grandma Hilda, who had also lived in Germany. That was a plus—instead of wearing a million beads and flowers and ruffles to appear large in that area, she could be herself. Or, she could be in a year or so. Not to overdo, of course. Some of Mama's friends looked like battleships.

As she came up to her house, Sally noticed a smart two-seater buggy. A horse tied to a hitching post grazed on the winter-bleached grass.

"Damn," she said out loud; no one could hear her. The rig belonged to Elvira Gottlieb. Apparently Mrs. Gottlieb had come to tea.

She greeted the horse, patting his nose. You couldn't hold it against a horse to whom he belonged. He nuzzled against her, whinnying that he was lonely and needed company. She ran one finger down his nose, whispered "Be good," and ran over to the field, waiting for the three Gottesman horses to come trotting toward her.

The two brown bay carriage horses, Elmer and Oswald, and her own special palomino filly, Stardust, rubbed eagerly against the fence, stomping a little with impatience. Sally put down her books and rummaged through her handbag, bringing out three sugar cubes. "There," she said, popping a sugar cube behind each horse's big, grinning teeth. She gave the bays each a kiss on the top of the nose and Stardust a hug. Then she went inside to face the Gottlieb ordeal.

The Gottesman house was comfortable, but not as large as some of the mansions that had been built with mining and merchant fortunes. The doctor was prosperous, but not wealthy. The house, built of red Colorado stone hewn in large blocks and trimmed with cream-colored wood, had a roomy front porch supported by posts carved into decorative spindles. A trellis, covered with last summer's dried vines, shielded one end of the porch from the sun, creating a delicious cavern on hot summer days where one could glide on the porch swing, read, and dream.

Sally opened the heavy oak front door with its stained glass window and tried to tiptoe through the front hall. But ecstatic yips from a buff-colored cocker spaniel gave her away.

"Down, Barney," she ordered, kneeing him lightly.

Barney was a slow learner. He kept jumping, needing a kiss. Finally, she kissed him on top of the head. He subsided, but it was too late. Her mother's silvery voice came from the parlor. "Sally dear, come and say hello to Mrs. Gottlieb."

Disgustedly, Sally thumped her books and package onto the marble-topped hall table. Dust flew into the air—Ingrid, the maid, was an indifferent duster. The ponderous black mahogany grandfather clock chimed five.

She sauntered into the parlor to confront The Gottlieb, as the guest was called behind her back. At first the room might seem overwhelming, with its heavy green velvet draperies, horsehair sofa with elaborately carved wood trim, red Brussels carpet, thick oak woodwork, and flowered wallpaper. But its fussiness and heaviness were a refuge from the Colorado winters; it made one feel safe somehow. In June the heavy draperies would be taken down and replaced with light muslin curtains and the carpet removed and beaten thoroughly and straw summer matting put down.

Clara Gottesman sat in a green armchair before the bay window. The glow of late afternoon filtering through lace curtains behind her brought out the reddish highlights in her thick chestnut hair drawn up to a knot on the top her head and covered with a little beribboned lace cap. Her mother made Sally think of the ivory figures she saw in the Chinese shops down on Wazee Street. Her skin was cream-colored and never became ruddy like that of the rest of her family. She had soft brown eyes and her nose—oh, how Sally envied her mother's nose—was perfectly straight.

In other words, Clara was a beauty. Young Doctor Gottesman, who had made his way west to Kansas City from Germany, had been enchanted by the lovely Clara. Much to her family's distress, he had convinced her to marry him and come with him to Denver, six hundred miles into the wilderness.

Awkwardly, Sally greeted Mrs. Gottlieb, a vast woman attired in violet watered silk with large double frills at the shoulder and leg-o'-mutton sleeves, puffed at the top, conspiring to make her look larger than she actually was. Her graying hair was arranged in a bush of curls at the front and drawn up into a side-swept chignon.

Sally bobbed a little curtsy, then remembered

that she wasn't a little girl anymore and sat down on a small hard chair facing the tea table.

"Sally," Mrs. Gottlieb acknowledged her, studying her with beady black eyes.

"I'm . . . I'm glad to see you, Mrs. Gottlieb." Sally stammered through the hostess pleasantries she had been carefully taught. "How is your daughter Gertrude and Mr. Gottlieb?" Mrs. Gottlieb's husband was one of the investors who had come from the east to manage the smelters.

Clara sniffed meaningfully.

"And your cold? I understand you had quite a cold last week."

"Better, thank you. The family is well." Mrs. Gottlieb reached out a beringed hand for another cookie.

Clara rang a silver bell and Ingrid appeared, somewhat dressed as a maid with a cap atop her flyaway straw-colored hair. Ingrid was a big farm girl recently arrived from Sweden. When she saw Sally she grinned and patted her bulging apron pocket from which an envelope protruded.

"Bring a cup for Sally," said Clara slowly, pointing at a cup and then Sally. "And more tea." She handed her the teapot. Ingrid, who was learning English with a flat Kansas accent from Clara, grinned and whisked the teapot away.

"You're late. Where were you?" Clara asked Sally.

Sally refrained from grabbing more than one

bread and butter sandwich, although the sandwiches were tiny and she was starved.

Ingrid reappeared with a porcelain cup and
saucer and the teapot. Once again she patted her
apron pocket.

"Yah," said Sally. Ingrid hurried away, giggling
into her hand.

"I stopped by Uncle Abraham's store to buy
material for my Purim costume," Sally explained.

Clara delicately lifted the teapot, offered more
tea to Mrs. Gottlieb, and then filled Sally's cup.
"How exciting. Could we see it?"

"No," Sally cried in alarm. Then, swiftly, "It's to
be a surprise. You know everything's spoiled if
you show off your costume ahead of time."

"I suppose so," Clara murmured uneasily. She
was constantly being surprised by Sally. A calm
peaceful woman, Clara had trouble coping with
her imaginative daughter and huge rambunctious
sons.

Mrs. Gottlieb squinted at Sally suspiciously.

Hastily, to change the subject, Sally exclaimed,
"The most awful thing! Aunt Frank came in while I
was in the store. She had been down on Market
Street . . ."

Mrs. Gottlieb's small mouth pursed disapprovingly. Clara looked distressed. Sally felt that she
had ventured into dangerous waters, but she could-
n't stop herself. "Two of the girls who lived there
took an overdose of morphine and nearly died.
Aunt Frank called Papa and he saved the girls' lives.

He was the hero . . ."

Her voice trailed off as Mrs. Gottlieb uttered a loud offended sniff. Her clifflike bosom heaved. "Really," she said. "I can't understand that Jacobs woman. Running to all the riffraff in town. Talk is that she's deranged."

"Frances does a lot of good," Clara ventured timidly.

For her part, Sally would have liked to hit Mrs. Gottlieb over the head with the nearest object. But one must be polite to one's guests.

The Gottlieb rumbled on. "The city is being overrun with human vermin." She drew into herself as if avoiding lice and cockroaches. "All those dirty lungers coming in looking for a quick cure for their filthy disease. They just get sent here from other cities that want to get rid of them. And those foreigners . . . Russians, and Chinese heathens swarming around Wazee."

Sally remembered distinctly that Mrs. Gottlieb owned a Ming dynasty vase which, she never tired of reminding people, "cost a fortune." It was on the tip of her tongue to remind her that the Chinese who had come to America to build the railroads were of the same race as the genius who had created her vase. She contented herself with saying, "The Chinese have been very much mistreated. They live in misery." While she had the opportunity, she added, "And I don't think it was fair to make the Indians move to Utah. This was their land. Just because gold and silver were found in Colorado."

Clara frowned. Once again Sally had gone beyond the boundaries of good taste for a young lady, who really should be seen and not heard.

Mrs. Gottlieb delivered a look of icy scorn. "These are inferior races. They don't know what's good for them."

Now even Clara was driven to reply. "It is written in the Torah that we must care for the stranger, as Abraham greeted the angels. Jews care for all people, because we have promised God to do so."

"Well, God did not live in Denver," said Mrs. Gottlieb righteously. Sally sputtered a tea-filled laugh into her napkin.

"Many of the poor who live in West Colfax are Jews," Clara reminded her guest. "We must take care of our own."

Mrs. Gottlieb heaved a wounded sigh. "I suppose so. But they are embarrassing with their beards and their sheitels and their crazy mixed-up German."

"Yiddish," said Clara. "It's a language of its own."

"May I be excused?" asked Sally. "I have a great deal of homework . . . Latin," she added, to impress Mrs. Gottlieb.

Safely out of the parlor, she rushed to the kitchen where Ingrid was peeling potatoes.

"You got a letter from Lars?" she asked, drawing up a wooden chair to the big table and taking up a peeler. "Yah." Ingrid drew out the letter and showed it to Sally.

"It's in Swedish."

"Oh, yah." Ingrid laughed. "He say . . . he say he New York."

"Oh, he came from Sweden." Sally bounced in excitement. "Will he come to Colorado?"

"Maybe. Need money." Ingrid put out her hands and pretended to be driving horses.

"Aha," said Sally. "He is a driver. A wagon?"

"Yah," said Ingrid.

Ingrid sighed. "Lars and me, we buy farm. Someday."

Sally leaned forward. "Ingrid, how do you know the right one?" She put her hand on her heart and made panting sounds and then pursed her lips in smacking kisses.

Ingrid whooped with laughter, throwing her apron over her face. "Is good," she said carefully. Solemnly, she put up two index fingers. "Is good, one like other. The same."

"The same," said Sally thoughtfully. "I have to find a boy like me. Somehow. Ingrid, let me show you something," and she unwrapped the parcel and brought out the costume material.

"Ah," said Ingrid, holding up the red net. "Is good. How you do it?"

Sally wrapped the net fabric around her legs to show the pants and then swirled the silver cloth around her waist. "Like so."

Ingrid put her hand to her mouth in shock.

"Where you wear this thing?"

"Purim Ball. Party." Sally got up and waltzed around the room.

"Ah, party," cried Ingrid joyously. She jumped to her feet and grabbed Sally's hands and pranced with her, singing a Swedish song, until they collapsed breathlessly in their chairs.

"One time long ago, some Jews lived in Persia," said Sally.

"Persia." Ingrid leaned forward as if by doing so she could understand English better. "Persia," she repeated. She had heard of Persia.

"Persia had a king named Ahasuerus, very stuck up. He sent away his first wife because she wouldn't come when he called her. Like a puppy. Like Barney." Sally patted Barney, who was snoozing at their feet.

"Barney no come. Here!" Ingrid banged and whistled. Barney opened one eye and then went back to sleep.

"Like Barney, Vashti no come," said Sally, and then shook her head. Who was teaching whom English? "So Ahasuerus got rid of Vashti. Then the silly king had no wife so he gathered all the girls in the kingdom to pick the prettiest. Who do you think was prettiest?"

"Most pretty, ah . . ." Ingrid leaned back in her chair and closed her eyes. Then they popped open. "Ah, prettiest. Sally!"

"Why, thank you, Ingrid," Sally laughed. "But this is a real story. Not a game. The prettiest was

Esther, a Jewish girl."

Ingrid stared at her earnestly. "Jewish. Yah. No ham."

Clara had explained to Ingrid that because this was a Jewish home they did not serve ham and bacon.

"I don't suppose Esther ate ham," Sally sighed. This was getting difficult. But she couldn't stop in the middle.

"Okay, now Esther is Queen. So, there was this terrible man, Haman. He wanted to kill the Jews and steal their things. He told the king lies about the Jews and the king ordered all the Jews to be hanged." Sally put her fingers around her neck and made choking sounds. Ingrid jumped up in alarm.

"Well, Esther's Uncle Mordecai heard all about that and he figured that with his niece being the queen, she might have influence. So he went to Esther and told her to go to the king and tell him how awful Haman was, what a liar. But Esther remembered what happened to Vashti. A queen not only had to come when she was called, but she wasn't allowed to come if she wasn't called."

"I not marry him," Ingrid decided.

"Me either. I don't want a man who orders me around. Anyway, Esther figured that she didn't want all her relatives to be killed so she took a chance. And she was so pretty, the king didn't mind. When he heard that Haman lied to him he got very mad and he had Haman hanged. So since then, all the Jews have fun on Purim."

"Purim." Ingrid rolled the new English word on her tongue.

"Hey-man," coached Sally.

"Hey man!" repeated Ingrid.

"Haman was a wicked wicked man!" sang Sally, pounding in time on the table with a wooden spoon.

"Haman vas vicked vicked."

"Haman was a wicked wicked man."

The two girls held hands again and danced a Swedish dance, singing at the tops of their voices, "Haman was a wicked man!"

"What's going on here?"

Hastily, Ingrid sat down and commenced peeling potatoes furiously.

Sally stuffed the costume material behind the potato bowl.

"I'm teaching Ingrid about Purim, Papa."

"I think they can hear you in New York," said Dr. Gottesman, bending to kiss his daughter on the cheek. He was a slim man, with thinning reddish blond hair combed straight across his head. His spade-shaped beard, just lightly flecked with gray, made him look very medical, but his deep blue eyes, just like Sally's, twinkled behind gold-rimmed spectacles.

"Papa, Aunt Frank told me about how you saved the two girls."

"Yes," he said. "Nasty business. They were probably too drunk to know what they were doing.

A waste. Such a waste of young lives."

"Is it wrong, do you think, Papa, for Aunt Frank to go there? With the bad women?"

He sighed. "It is not very safe. But your Aunt Frances thinks she can heal the world. And to hear her speak, she can. But she needs more help."

"They say she can talk a wooden Indian out of his cigars."

Dr. Gottesman smiled. "That she can. Frances is quite a speaker. So, you are getting in the mood for the big Purim Ball, eh? What costume will you wear?"

"It's a surprise," said Sally primly. "And you, what will you wear?"

"I think I shall come as a medical doctor and I will wear my brown suit. I'm too old for costumes. By the way, your brothers write that they will both be home for the party. It should be a wild weekend."

‧‧‧‧ *Chapter 3*

  With Sally squeezed between her brothers
Ephraim and Simon, the Gottesman buggy clip-
clopped toward Temple Emanuel. Both young
men were over six feet tall and muscular; they took
up a lot of room. Ephraim, who was studying law
at the University of Colorado in Boulder, had flam-
ing red hair that stood up in a stubborn cliff no matter how he slicked it down. Simon, a year younger,
a student at the new School of Mines in Golden,
had inherited his mother's dark hair and brown
eyes.
  Gaslit street lights gave the evening a golden
look, reflected in the soft gas headlights of passing

vehicles. Although it was still necessary to use lap robes, there was a certain tang to the air; once again Colorado was stirring, to bring forth spring. There was a faint odor of flower bulbs bursting and sending points of green above the earth, of sap beginning to move in the trees, of leaf buds becoming moist and alive.

Sally felt a curious excitement; it seemed as though a secret bell was chiming, inviting her to come and solve a mystery. She imagined she was going around a bend in the road and beyond that, hidden from her now, there was something wonderful. The stars so far overhead could see everything. They knew what her future would be, around the corner, behind the mountain. She was earthbound and could not see, but she knew it was there.

She shivered.

Ephraim drew the lap robe more tightly around her. "Chilly, baby sister?"

She gave him a sharp nudge with her elbow. "No, the baby is not cold."

He pulled at her coat. "Let's see what you're wearing."

"No." She jerked away. "You're not supposed to look before the ball."

"You know what I'm wearing." He was dressed as a pirate. Ephraim always came as a pirate.

Simon straightened his tattered high silk hat, rescued from the rubbish bin. Charcoal amplified his own tiny scrub mustache. "What's Carrie wearing?"

"I have no idea," Sally said demurely.

"Yes you do!" Simon almost shook her, but remembered in time that his bratty sister was now a young lady, at least in years if not in actions.

"Don't fight, children," said Clara from the front seat.

"Mama still thinks we're children," laughed Ephraim. "Ya ya, Simon took my ball. Take that, Simon," and he pretended to hit his brother.

Simon replied with a mock uppercut.

Sally, rocking between them, felt seasick.

"I'll tell you what," she said. "Let's pretend we're grown-ups."

"Splendid idea. Miss Sally, will you kindly tell me what Miss Carrie is wearing so I can be first in line asking her to dance?"

Sally sighed. "She is coming as the Spirit of Spring. I believe she's wearing green."

"That would figure," muttered Ephraim.

"Um," said Simon, "As long as your friend Carrie is mentioned . . ."

"You mentioned her," said Sally tartly.

"I declare, Sally, you have a sharp tongue," her mother commented. "Men don't like that. They want a girl to be soft and, er, pliable."

The brothers laughed and Dr. Gottesman chuckled.

"Did I say something wrong?" asked Clara, bewildered.

Her husband reached over and patted her hand. "No, dear, you are perfectly right. Sally, sometimes the wisest use of the English language is to keep your mouth shut."

"Oh shoot," murmured Sally. Her family, all four of them, were always down on her, trying to make her into some kind of model frilly simpering girl. Just to make men like her. Well, she didn't care if men didn't like her.

But she kept silent. Besides, she did care if men liked her.

"As I was saying, Miss Sally. Have you ever had any conversations with Miss Carrie involving me?"

Sally and Carrie had had numerous discussions regarding Simon. In fact, Carrie was obsessed with Simon. She wanted to know his favorite foods and colors, what he was like as a little boy. When Sally told her how Simon had once fallen out of a tree and broken his arm, Carrie cried.

"No," said Sally. "I can't recall ever discussing you with my friend Carrie. We discuss more elevating matters."

"Clothes. 'Oh did you see that gown in Joslin's window? It was exquizzit! I shall make my Papa buy it for me.'" Ephraim spoke in a high squeaky voice. Sally gave him another unladylike elbow jab.

"She doesn't even know I'm alive," said Simon glumly.

It suddenly occurred to Sally that if Carrie married Simon, she would be her sister. What fun!

"She likes you. She likes you very much. She told me."

The fact that Sally had just betrayed a confidence she had promised upon pain of death never to reveal did not bother her. Sometimes you simply had to help life along.

Suddenly the gentle gaslight was changed to a flash of brilliance as they passed a cross street. The horses reared a little and Dr. Gottesman clucked soothing words to them.

"What happened here?" exclaimed Ephraim.

"They've put in electric street lights on New Haven Street," said Dr. Gottesman. "It's said that some day the whole city will be lit up with Mr. Edison's remarkable invention. People will even have electric lights in their houses. A great boon. With such bright light, you can read at night without straining your eyes."

"How does it work?" asked Clara.

Simon, the engineer, was eager to explain. He was still deep into a discussion of filaments and magnetos and new words like amperes and watts and volts, when the buggy drew up to the temple.

Temple Emanuel, which had been born as a burial society needed by the handful of Jewish pioneers who had come in 1859 with the gold-seekers, was now one of the most beautiful structures in Denver. Occupying the corner of Curtis and 24th Streets, it was an impressive brick building trimmed in stonework, described as Moorish in design, with arched windows. At the two front corners were steeples ninety feet tall, each with a sharply pointed roof surmounted by a Star of David. The main sanctuary seated five hundred people, and it had other rooms housing a thriving religious school. The temple was part of the Reform movement—liberal Judaism originating in Germany. In 1881 a more orthodox synagogue, Ohava Emunu, had been established for more traditional worshipers. Other, smaller congregations had been founded by the increasing number of Eastern European Yiddish-speaking Jews.

The street in front of the temple was a tangle of buggies, impatient horses, shouting drivers, and excited young people swarming into the temple's banquet hall. Shepherded by adults dressed in evening clothes, they were a strange lot, mustached Hamans, glittering King Ahasueruses, bespangled Queen Esthers, a few sober Mordecais, and those who had abandoned Purim altogether—pirates, Gypsies, sailors, and miners complete with cardboard pickaxes.

And then there was Vashti, Ahasuerus' first wife.

In the girls' cloakroom, Carrie, looking lovely in green chiffon with a garland of artificial apple blossoms around her head, squealed. "Sally, it's splendid! Turn around."

Sally adjusted the curls emerging from her silver bandanna, swished her silver belt, and twirled in velvet slippers. "Wiggle!" ordered Carrie.

As Sally obliged, other girls from the Confirmation class—Lena Wald, Rose Loeb, and Lillie Kramer—clustered around, giggling.

"Girls, this is not a medicine show," Sally scolded. "It's a protest. Vashti was thrown out because she defied the king. I believe a woman should not have to obey her husband."

"And who should she obey?" asked Lena, choking with mirth.

"Herself," said Sally and did another pirouette.

"Sally, you're crazy," said Lillie. "Women can't make decisions. That's why we must have husbands, to take care of us."

Lillie was a skinny girl with pale calculating eyes, a long nose, and a thin mouth. Dressed in cascades of pink ruffles and carrying a stick surmounted with a star, she was supposed to be a good fairy, but she seemed more like a discontented fairy to Sally, a thin junior Elvina Gottlieb.

Sally stared at her in disgust. Lillie stared back, her nostrils flaring. The two were enemies.

Rose, who was dressed as Queen Esther, broke the tension with mock weeping. "I, Queen Esther, am being attacked by my husband's first wife. What did I ever do to deserve such a thing? My mother told me to marry a nice Jewish boy."

In gales of laughter, the girls trooped into the ballroom.

The room, usually used for religious school assemblies, was draped with blue and white streamers. There was a fragrance of coffee and punch and fresh hamentaschen—cakes baked by the ladies of the temple in the shape of Haman's hat—and the cloying mixture of perfumes. Amid the babble of many voices, small children ran around twirling groggers (noisemakers) and shouting "Down with Haman!" The orchestra, the best in Denver, colorful in band-concert uniforms of red with gold epaulets, was playing a waltz, and couples whirled around the center of the room.

A group of boys lounged around, pretending to be interested in man-talk or just looking uncomfortable. When the girls arrived, an electric current, like those described by Simon, seemed to ripple through the male group. The girls kept to themselves, pretending that the boys didn't exist.

Several adults, sitting on the sidelines, gasped when Sally walked by. She could hear the buzz of their comments and felt embarrassed. But it was too late now. Anyhow, the pants were wonderfully comfortable. No wonder sometimes she wanted to be a boy! They wore such comfortable clothes, and they always got to be the bosses. But then, they were noisy and constantly had to prove something, like going off to dangerous wars and getting shot. It was better to be a girl, in the long run.

Simon detached himself from a group of older fellows and came sidling over, a strange glow on his face as he stared at Carrie. Carrie melted into a demure maiden.

"Miss Rosenthal, may I have the honor of this dance?" Simon's face had turned red.

Shyly, Carrie placed her hand on his arm and let him accompany her to the dance floor.

The other girls sighed. Romance.

The girls passed by the seated adults, ambling, as if by chance, toward the boys. "Sally!" Her father's steely tone meant come right away. Sally detached herself from her friends and walked meekly to where her parents were sitting with the Jacobses.

"My stars, Sally," exclaimed Clara. "Where did you get that outfit?"

"I made it myself," said Sally virtuously. "On your sewing machine."

"It's indecent!" Clara looked as though she were about to cry.

Looking almost pretty in beaded black silk, Aunt Frank regarded Sally intently. It seemed to Sally that Aunt Frank's "listening ears," now adorned with jet earrings, were trying to hear exactly what Sally had in mind when she designed the costume. A prank, yes, but something deeper.

Sally always felt safe when Aunt Frank was near, as if a friend was holding her hand when she ventured down an unknown road.

Her parents were not concerned with unknown roads. "I feel disgraced. Everyone is here . . . the Anfengers, the Londoners, the Appels. How can I face them when my daughter has made such a spectacle of herself?" Clara took a lace handkerchief out of her little evening bag and sniffed loudly.

"Clara, stop it," Frances scolded. "The child

looks enchanting, and those pants are wonderful to dance in. Turn around, Sally."

Slowly, Sally obeyed.

"You look like a dancing girl at the Last Chance Saloon," said Dr. Gottesman.

"And what would you know of the Last Chance Saloon?" his wife muttered, trying to stifle a laugh that spoiled her tears.

"Medical visits only, my dear. Purely professional."

Always the politician, Wolfe Londoner—round face exuding love for all, brushy mustache, eyes twinkling, and neat bow tie—came by, accompanied by his wife, a head taller than he, and genially shook hands.

"And who have we here?" he said, regarding Sally. "One of the dancing girls from King Solomon's harem?"

King Solomon's harem. That would have been almost respectable. No one had thought of that.

"No, Mr. Londoner," said Sally. "I'm Vashti, King Ahasuerus' first wife, the one he discarded for Esther."

Mr. Londoner reared back his head in a hearty laugh. "Clever! Our children are full of imagination, eh Sig?"

Dr. Gottesman nodded in agreement. People seldom disagreed with Wolfe Londoner; he was always so positive and expansive.

"Beautiful costume," murmured Mrs. Londoner

as they moved on to shake more hands.

"Why Vashti?" asked Frances.

"I think she was unfairly treated," said Sally. "The king told her to come, just to show her off to his friends. But maybe Vashti had something more important to do. He could have asked her nicely and then listened to her explanation."

Frances nodded thoughtfully. "That's so. I never thought of that. How old are you, Sally?"

"I'll be sixteen in September." Aunt Frank knew how old she was. She was about to make a point.

"I think she's old enough to come down to our suffrage meetings," Frances said to Sally's mother. "We need the young girls. They're the future and that's when women will get the vote."

Clara, devoted to the suffrage cause, had been one of the women who tried unsuccessfully to get women's right to vote included in the Colorado state constitution in 1877.

"We'll see," she said. "All right, Sally. Go and have a good time. I don't suppose you look any more outlandish than others here."

Sally moved back toward the crowded dance floor, where Gypsies and Esthers and Hamans and kings were tripping around the floor in a high-kicking polka. Voices had become shrill with excitement, groggers in the hands of over-excited children continued to make their ratchety sound. The band, consisting mainly of brass instruments and a banging piano, sent the music ricocheting and echoing from wooden beams. Steam heat came sizzling through ceiling pipes. Sweat formed under Sally's tightly wound headband.

The scene was making her dizzy and she felt quite alone. She searched for her friends but they were all dancing. Carrie, her flower garland askew, was firmly holding hands with Simon as they pranced by. Along the side of the room, seated with stiff hopeful smiles, were the wallflowers. Sally whisked away from them.

Suddenly she felt a tap on her shoulder. "May I have the honor?"

She turned and faced Nathan Wald, Lena's brother. As a little kid coming to play with her brothers, he had been known as "Nat the Fat," but now the fat had melted and he was tall and had curly dark hair and dimples and deep brown eyes and a wonderful dusky rose complexion.

The polka was over and the band had started playing a waltz, "When the Leaves Begin to Fall." Sally drifted into Nat's arms and they moved, it seemed to her, on a cloud supported only by the music, around and around. The harem pants were a wonder . . . her legs felt so free, it seemed as if she could dance forever, following Nat's lead just ever so lightly.

"You dance extremely well," he murmured. "When did you get so pretty?"

"Thanks," she stammered. After all those afternoons practicing with Carrie and Lena how to flirt with a man, everything had fled from her memory.

There was something about laying a handkerchief against the right cheek to say "Yes," but you couldn't do that while you were whirling around a dance floor.

He grinned. "You smell good."

That meant he wanted her to move closer. He had bay rum on his face; she recognized that. But it would be silly to tell him he smelled good too. "My mother's attar of roses." Now that was childish, admitting that she had filched her mother's rose water.

She flushed, partly from the heat and partly from the confusion of not knowing what to say next.

"It's very warm," he remarked. "Want to stop?"

"Yes, no." She wanted to dance forever, but she was hot.

"Let's get some punch and hamentaschen." He took her hand and led her toward the refreshment table. Ceremoniously, he poured pink punch into a crystal cup and handed her a hamentaschen on a little plate. It was the poppy seed kind, which she detested, but she felt it would be unladylike to ask him to change it for prune.

"What are you doing now?" she asked primly as they sat down at a small table.

Lazily, he crossed his legs. "Learning to be a gentleman at Denver University."

"You haven't chosen a profession?"

He laughed. "My papa is rich. I don't need a profession. Just follow in Pater's footsteps."

The Walds had a large freighting business and

lived in one of the mansions in Curtis Park. But, as Mama would say, it was in bad taste to mention it.

He focused his dazzling smile, all dimples, on her and asked, almost tenderly as if she were some fragile being, "Would you like another hamentaschen?"

Sally knew she was supposed to say, "Oh no I couldn't." After all, her delicate female constitution would not permit her to overeat—in public, anyhow. But she was starved and she really wanted a prune hamentaschen. "Yes, please." She looked up and him and blinked a little, the way she and the girls had practiced. As he turned toward the table, she yelled, "Nat, a prune one please," and then hastily slapped her hand over her mouth. A lady never yelled, at least in public. Across the room, she saw Rose and Lillie whispering. They were staring at her and at Nat. Lillie looked as if she'd just swallowed a pickle.

Come to think of it, Nat was quite a catch. So handsome and, after all, his papa was very rich.

While Sally and Nat munched on their hamentaschen, the band took a break. Mr. Louis Anfenger, president of the temple, made a welcoming speech. Over in a corner, Aunt Frank was conferring with Otto Mears, the famous "Pathfinder of the San Juans," the man who had built the roads to the mines through Colorado mountains. Now he was president of the Rio Grande and Southern Railroad. A small, large-nosed man, a Russian Jew, he seldom smiled. But he had a liking for Frances

Jacobs and contributed generously to her charities.

The music started again—this time a lively gallop. Nat held out his hand and Sally took it and they went out to the dance floor. As they romped through the dance, she felt as if her feet had taken wings. All around her was a kaleidoscope of color and sound. Faces floated by, Carrie looking starry-eyed, Simon utterly foolish, Ephraim with Lena, Nat's sister . . . their parents, forgetting their dignity and rushing, trying to keep up with the music . . . Frances and Abraham Jacobs, laughing and swinging their arms like a couple of children.

This, decided Sally, was the most wonderful night of her life.

And when it was over, Nat held her hand a little longer than was necessary and whispered, "I want to see you again."

Chapter 4

The rains had diminished. Colorado displayed
crabapple blossoms and tulips and swelling leaf
buds. It was May.

Rabbi Mendes de Sola, plodding through an afternoon in a stuffy classroom, tried to instill some spiritual knowledge into fourteen teenagers, the confirmation class. He was a placid, chubby man with
a small mustache, sixty-seven years old.

Born and raised in Amsterdam, Holland, to a dis-
tinguished Sephardic family originally from Spain,
Rabbi de Sola had served in Curacao, in the Dutch
West Indies, before coming to the United States.
Rabbi de Sola didn't believe in arguing; whatever
the trustees of the Temple decided was fine with
him. The rabbi was devoted to Reform Judaism and

to worship in English. He'd wanted to change the *Kaddish*, the prayer for the dead, into English instead of Hebrew, but the Board members, liberal as they all were, had put their collective foot down. You didn't tamper with *Kaddish*. That was fine with Rabbi de Sola.

He had secrets, Sally decided. Sometimes while he was lecturing them, he grew thoughtful, as if he were considering something that had nothing to do with what he was saying.

Now, as Joe Weinberg and Dave Ginsburg, who generally sat in back, occupied themselves by throwing hard little paper pellets at Lillie's neck, and Lena Wald drew pictures of impossibly elaborate ball gowns for the amusement of Rose Loeb, the rabbi droned on. The topic was the Ten Commandments.

"Confirmation is always on *Shavuot*, the celebration of the first fruits," he said. "Can anyone tell me why?"

The class stared at him blankly.

"Stop it," shrilled Lillie as a hard pellet hit her neck.

"Boys!" The rabbi's chubby face tried to look severe. He advanced on Dave with a ruler as if he were about to strike him. Rabbi de Sola had never been known to hit anybody. Dave, a skinny boy with big ears and comical eyebrows, clasped his hands in a caricature of contrition. The girls giggled.

Sighing, the rabbi returned to the front of the room and continued the discussion, if it could be called that. "First fruits?"

Miriam Millstein, a small girl with big dark eyes who always seemed to be surprised by what was going on, raised a timid hand. The rabbi smiled at her. He was fond of Miriam.

"Because we're the young people. The first fruits."

"Very good," the rabbi beamed.

Milton Silverman, a tall boy with abundant dark hair parted on the side and challenging blue eyes, waggled his hand.

"Yes?" said the rabbi, resigned to argument.

"Why would we celebrate fruits in June? Peaches are ripe in the summer and apples in the fall."

"We are talking about a different climate— Palestine, not Colorado," the rabbi said patiently. "Anyhow, this discussion is not about produce."

"You said . . ." mumbled Milton.

"That will be enough, Silverman. Miriam has told us that our first fruits are our children. Our wonderful young people, the hope of Israel." Meditatively, he recited, "The first of the first fruits of your ground you shall bring to the house of the Lord your God." He stared at the class. Someone laughed nervously. The rabbi ignored the laughter.

"Now," he said loudly, opening a large Bible. "*Shavuot* also celebrates the Ten Commandments and therefore you will each recite a suitable essay regarding one of the commandments. Since there are fourteen of you and only ten commandments, I have divided four of them—kill, steal, false witness, and covet—so that two of you will share." He brought out slips of paper and handed them to the students.

Sally read her Commandment, "Honor your father and your mother, that your days may be long in the land which the Lord your God gives you." There followed a paragraph about respecting and obeying one's parents.

That set her to thinking. Suppose a person had parents who were thieves, or were cruel. Should you obey them when they tell you to do something bad? She thought of the novel by Charles Dickens, *Oliver Twist.* Fagan told the boys to steal . . . but, then, he wasn't their parent.

All of this went around and around in her mind as the rabbi read the Commandments from his Bible. This happened to Sally sometimes. Thoughts came to her and wondering and there was no one to talk to about them. The only person she could really talk to was Aunt Frank, who listened to her as if she were an adult. But even that was mostly about practical things, not ideas.

Rabbi de Sola had put down the Bible, sighing.

Sally watched him intently. The rabbi was looking out the window at the vivid May garden and wishing he was there. And he was looking, not directly, but from the corner of his eye, at the clock, where fifteen minutes more remained of this imprisonment with unresponsive youngsters.

He was melancholy. He was homesick.

He sat down and crossed one leg over the other and said, in a warm unrabbinic voice, "In my homeland there lived a Jewish man . . ."

Sally was startled. She had read his mind!

A subtle shifting went through the class as though they were awakening from a collective dream. When the rabbi told his stories, about Holland or about the tropical paradise Curacao, they listened.

"This man was a humble person, a lens grinder. But while he did his monotonous work, his mind was busy. He thought a lot about Gott. And the more he thought, the less he felt that Gott was a man vid a beard who sat on a throne in heaven. As he looked out the vindow of his little cottage he saw the birds fly into the trees and build their nests and the clouds come rolling by, releasing the rain that kept things alive. It's rather damp in Holland . . . below sea level, you know. The opposite of Colorado.

"Anyhow," the rabbi continued, "this man decided that Gott is in everything. That is called 'Pantheism.' And so," the rabbi's voice went high. "He labored long and hard and wrote a book about his belief. And because what he believed was different, the people of Holland were very angry. They went to the Jews and said 'Look what this Jew has written. He is evil, a heretic.' And the Jews, even though they have always felt that a man's thoughts are sacred, bowed down to the people of Holland. As I think I told you, the Dutch velcomed my ancestors when they ran away from the Inquisition in Spain. So the Jews felt they owed something to the Dutch."

He paused.

"What did they do?" asked Carrie breathlessly.

"They excommunicated him, in the year 1656. That means they wouldn't let him be a Jew anymore. No Jew could have anything to do with him or help him. Their behavior was shameful!"

"What was his name?" asked Sally.

"Spinoza. Baruch Spinoza. A great man." The rabbi got up and wrote the name on the blackboard. "When he was only forty-four years old, he died of tuberculosis, like so many Jews who have come to our city for help."

"All right," he said. "Class dismissed."

Leaving the building, the girls buzzed about the dresses they were to wear for confirmation. But Sally didn't feel like talking about dresses. Walking alongside her friends, she separated herself from them through silence. All the way home on the horsecar she sat quietly . The windows of the car were open and a breeze seemed to embrace her with the scent of flowers.

When she reached home, she could not bear to stay in the house. She put her books away and changed into riding knickers and ran outside, saddled up Stardust, and galloped toward the mountains.

She rode up a familiar path to a small foothill and dismounted. Tying the filly to a tree where she could treat herself to tender mosses, Sally went to a gnarled old pine tree and seated herself, hunched up against its trunk.

The hillside was beginning to turn pastel with new mountain flowers, delicate bells and lupines and the tall yellow cactus flowers called "miners' candles." Below her was the valley, pale green with emerging wheat, and beyond that, cattle roamed. In the distance, a tiny string of freight cars steamed toward Colorado Springs and Pueblo, the locomotive belching coal smoke.

The peaks of distant mountains caught the rays of the western sun, and suddenly there was a dazzle of light atop the peaks.

Sally caught her breath and hugged her arms against her chest. She imagined that sitting beside her was the lens grinder, Baruch Spinoza, and together they had the same thought. "It is all God." God is in the mountains and in the streams, and even . . . she caught her breath . . . in me.

As she remounted Stardust and rode, slowly this time, down the path, she felt a searing longing that might be, she wondered, love.

"I love you, world," she shouted. And aspen leaves made papery sounds in reply.

Purple and rose clouds crowded out the sun, but suddenly brilliant rays shot through and illuminated the valley with a silver light. As Stardust stepped along under a lax rein, Sally half-closed her eyes, dreaming. Somewhere out there in the world, she thought, is a person who wonders, like me.

Two days before confirmation, Clara fretted, "I don't know why we offered our home for the confirmation party," as she supervised the delivery of a tent and extra chairs and long tables where the refreshments would be served. "We don't have room for that crowd in the house and who knows what will happen to the weather on June second. It can rain, blow cold, develop a heat wave, even snow."

"But then, my dear, if we wait a few minutes, it'll change. That's the advantage of early June. If you don't like the weather, wait a minute. Anyhow, we have the tent where people can go if there are a few spatters." Dr. Gottesman reached toward a heaping plate of cookies and snatched one as his wife stared anxiously out of the window, watching for dangerous clouds.

Colorado did its early June thing on June first, blowing and storming, but the next morning the sun returned, beaming as if to say "Miss me?"

As the family drove to the temple, spangles of raindrops floated from the trees, tiny rainbows winking out in the dry air. Sally sat gingerly at the edge of her seat, afraid to muss her dress. Designed by dressmaker Eleanor Flanagan, it was the most elegant thing Sally had ever owned. White lace in a pattern of open ovals, it had a ruffled collar and paniers over the hips and a small cascading white bustle that she was trying not to crumple. The only drawback was that all the other girls had the same dress. Mrs. Flanagan and her helpers had vowed "never again," after trying to please seven girls, some chubby, some too thin, some short and some tall, and all clamoring and complaining. Carrie, who had read a peculiar account in the newspaper of a girl in San Francisco who couldn't stand being fitted for dresses and always fainted, staged a mock fainting episode. Lillie Kramer pouted, saying the dress didn't suit her figure. "What figure?" muttered Sally to Lena. "She looks like a stick."

At the entrance to the sanctuary, the girls stood shyly, ready to be consecrated. Their hair was brushed back and shining and tied with white bows, and there were bows on their shoes. The boys, dressed alike in dark suits and white bow ties, fidgeted.

The rabbi, it seemed to Sally, offered an endless Shavuot service with many "Oh Lord, bless us and our children" prayers uttered in his Dutch accent. Finally, the organ pealed and the choir, invisible in a latticed balcony opposite the bima and the ark, sang with angelic fervor.

"Now," said Evelyn Jacobs, in charge of the procession. As the organ pumped away, the confirmands marched in pairs of boys and girls, separated at the altar, and came up either side of the bima. Solemn, looking scratchy in their high starched collars, the temple dignitaries sat on carved wooden chairs. There was Herman Silver, the new temple president, the secretary, Benjamin Wisebart, brother of Frances Jacobs, and Abraham Sands, the treasurer.

One by one the confirmands came to the pulpit, made their Ten Commandments speech, and received a Certificate of Confirmation, signed by the dignitaries and containing the temple motto, taken from the one hundred and nineteenth Psalm, "Thou art my portion, O Lord. I have said that I would keep thy words."

At last it was over. Sally thought that she sounded screechy but the family claimed she was the best.

"I hope you will remember the words you said about honoring your father and mother," said Clara piously in the buggy going home. "Do you think it's going to rain? That cloud over there. It can grow."

It didn't rain. The Jewish elite of Denver, and many non-Jews as well, swarmed over the spacious Gottesman land. The tables were piled high with plum cake and barbecued chicken and home-baked *challah* and ices and punch. The rabbi blessed the bread and the wine. There were tedious speeches from temple officers and from representatives of Denver's government and business circles, who somehow connected the need for free coinage of silver, vital to Colorado's mining interests, with the confirmation of fourteen Jewish teenagers.

Sally skirted around a circle of men—Louis Anfenger, Charles Schayer, Samuel Cole, Wolfe Londoner, and the morose Otto Mears—most of them members of the exclusive Pioneer Society, people who had come to Colorado before 1860. She liked to eavesdrop when the oldtimers talked. Some of them had been peddlers, toiling with packs of merchandise into the tiny mining camps in the mountains.

One man laughed, "I dragged my stuff to the top of the hill, but when I started down, the pack was so heavy, I was out of balance, so I just rolled it down the hill."

"We were all young then," sighed Mr. Schayer, taking another piece of cake.

Otto Mears, in a rare mellow mood in the company of old cronies, reminisced in his heavy Yiddish accent. "Do you know how I built my first road? I had a grist mill, with a vooden vheel, tied with rawhide." And he described a large wheel with his hands. "I ground good flour from mine vheat . . . I had a little farm, you know, homestead. But I ain't got customers. So I look for customers. There, over the hill, in the Arkansas Valley there was plenty people, looking for gold. How to get the vheat to the customers? There was no vagon road. So," he spread out his hands and shrugged his shoulders. "I built one, mit axes and shovels. You don't give up in this world. You do vhat you vant to do."

The other men, each of whom had his own hardship story, nodded.

Sally, lingering discreetly behind a nearby bush, waited eagerly for more stories, but she was interrupted by a tap on the shoulder. "Come on, let's dance. The fiddler's started."

Nat Wald dragged her away toward the music. "Why do you want to listen to those old codgers?"

"I think they're interesting, especially Mr. Mears. He's an amazing man. Do you know what he wants to do? He says they should cover the dome of the new state house with gold. That would be something!"

"Vhat?" Laughing, Nat imitated Mears' accent.

"He's a thoughtful man," Sally continued. "Interested in the things my Aunt Frank is doing. He doesn't live in the past; he cares about people."

"Crazy Frances!" Nat scoffed. "How come she didn't come to your party?"

Sally walked a little ahead of him, offended. She didn't want to quarrel with Nat, but she didn't want Aunt Frank insulted either. He hurried up behind her and grabbed her hand.

She decided to let the matter drop. What was the point of describing to Nat the good work Frances did? He'd only say Sally was crazy too. But she wondered what had happened to the Jacobses.

A lanky caller with a red kerchief around his neck and wearing a cowboy hat twanged out square dance calls.

"Comin' out tonight, comin' out tonight, Red

River Gal," sang the caller, scraping his fiddle.

"And y'all bow to yer partners, do-si-do, and then a grand right and left."

Sally wound in and out, touching right and left hands, all the while looking out for Frances and Abraham. If they were here, they'd be dancing. Frances never missed a dance.

"Back to your darling," said the caller. Nat grabbed Sally and twirled her around. "Promenade." As his arm went around her waist, he whispered, "You were the prettiest."

"Thank you," she said. "But I think my speech was a little shrill. My voice seemed to go up."

"A little shrill, yes," he agreed, grinning. He twirled her again.

Lillie Kramer, in the next square, dancing with Dave Ginsburg, looked around at Nat with an enticing smile. During the promenade, she wiggled a little more than necessary and then smiled at him again, inclining her head to make sure he was watching. "Lillie's quite a wiggler," Sally remarked.

"That she is," he said with interest.

Sally was alarmed. Lillie had set out to get Nat for no other reason than he was interested in her. Well, also because he was very good-looking and, as he often said, his Papa was rich.

She looked up at him with an admiring smile. Two could play this game. No little nasty stick girl was going to take a boy away from her.

But where, oh where, were the Jacobses?

A boy came riding into the yard on horseback. He seemed to be in a hurry. He ran over to Dr. Gottesman, who got up, ran into the house for his doctor bag, hitched up the buggy, and rode after the boy on horseback.

Aunt Frank and Uncle Abraham! Maybe they had been in an accident.

"Excuse me," she said abruptly, and left Nat standing there at the start of a new call. As she ran toward her mother, she noticed through the corner of her eye, that Lillie Kramer had unceremoniously left Dave and taken Nat's hand.

"The little bitch," Sally muttered. Sometimes big brothers educated you, teaching words that just fit the occasion.

Sally's mother, making sure that everyone had enough to eat, looked remarkably calm. Maybe there hadn't been a terrible accident after all. Sally slowed down.

"Where did Papa go?" she asked her mother.

Clara turned with a half-exasperated smile. "It's Frances!" she exclaimed. "If there's trouble, she'll find it even if she's going to a party. They were on their way here when they saw a poor woman on the street, hemorrhaging. Frances sent for your father." She handed Sally a tray. "Honey, please pass around the fruit tarts."

Sally passed around fruit tarts. Lillie Kramer, all wiggles and giggles, did do-si-does and promenades with the boy Sally considered her own, and Sally fumed. "Mr. Londoner, have you tried my mother's fruit tarts?"

The merry little man took one. "And how is Vashti today?" He never forgot. The man was a born politician.

"Very well, sir. Try the cherry preserves. That's the best."

An hour later, her father's buggy drew up. Sally went to see what had happened.

"Poor woman. She spoke only Yiddish. She collapsed in the street and we took her to the hospital—gloomy, stuffy place. No place for tuberculosis. Clara, we must have a decent hospital for these patients, particularly those who are penniless. Good clean beds, fresh air, good food. It's the only way we know how to treat the damn disease."

"Yes, dear," said Clara. "Go wash up. You're a sight."

The fiddler and caller had taken a break and the dancers flocked to the refreshment table for drinks. Sally stationed herself behind the table by the punch bowl. When Nat and Lillie came, she flashed a warm and loving smile at them. "Punch?" She ladled out a cup for Nathan, and another for Lillie, a bit too full.

"Ooh," said Lillie as a drop fell on her dress.

"It was so nice of you to take my place, dear," beamed Sally. She took Nat's hand. "Have you seen Mama's roses? They're early this year." As Lillie frantically tried to brush the spot from her dress, Sally led Nat to the rose garden, not yet in bloom, in the back of the house.

He gulped down his punch and unceremoniously grabbed her about the waist, planting his mouth against hers.

"Oh, how could you?" she shrieked, and pushed him away.

"Come on. You wanted it. Why are we here?"

Running her tongue over her upper lip, Sally looked at him. "I'm a virtuous Jewish girl."

"That's the best kind," he said huskily and pulled her close again. This time she didn't resist. His mouth was warm against hers and that flying feeling, like what she felt when she galloped Stardust across the field, came over her.

Maybe love?

Suddenly, a buggy drove into the yard. At last— the Jacobses. They alighted from the carriage, followed by a tattered figure.

"Who's the scarecrow?" Nat wondered.

"It's a boy," Sally snapped. An unfortunate person should not be the object of a jeer. She walked toward the newcomers, and Nat trailed behind her. The boy was about eighteen—actually a young man—and he was the filthiest, hungriest-looking person she'd ever seen. Embarrassed, but with pride, standing very straight, he looked around at the crowd.

Suddenly, his eyes lighted on her. She was standing there in a white lace dress and he was dressed in rags, gaunt, with a fuzz of whiskers, wearing shoes with rags stuffed in them to cover the holes in the soles. And they looked at each other.

His eyes were green, alive with intelligence. He seemed startled, staring at her as if he recognized her.

Out of nowhere, the memory of Ingrid holding up two index fingers, flashed into her mind. She took a step forward. She had a crazy urge to ask him what he thought of Spinoza.

Then, astonished at her own insanity, she clutched Nat's hand. The boy looked away.

"This is Daniel Rabinowitz," Aunt Frank was saying to Clara. "His mother collapsed on the sidewalk. Do you think we could get him something to eat?"

"Of course," said Clara. She looked around at the refreshments. "I don't think fruit tarts will do. Come along, Daniel," she said briskly. "We'll see if we can find you a nice plate of pot roast. And maybe some chicken soup left over from Shabbos. You like chicken soup?"

"Yes," said the boy. "Denk you."

As he followed her mother, his eyes caught Sally's again. He did not shuffle like a beggar, but swaggered a little, striding briskly, a person who knew where he was going.

Sally hardly heard Nat say, "We're all going skating down at the rink tomorrow. Want to come?"

She nodded abstractedly. "Yes." But the yes wasn't for Nat. It was for the unkempt boy who had just gone into the house.

wwwww *Chapter* **5**

Nat Wald bent to clamp the wheels to Sally's skate shoes. "You have pretty ankles," he murmured.

"Thank you." Sally spoke in what she and Carrie called the "chocolate mint" voice . . . if you thought about candy melting in the mouth your voice came out with a rich mellow tone, not squeaky, or girlishly silly, but inviting. Seductive. The girls spent hours rehearsing the fine points of flirtation when they were supposed to be conjugating Latin verbs. The voice especially. Get rid of the tomboy stridence she'd picked up from her brothers. Be soft and kittenish. Smile. As Nat helped her to her feet, she tried that, the slow arching smile. He looked at her with dazzled admiration. She was getting the hang of it.

Carrie seemed to have abandoned flirtation. She and Simon just gazed at each other. They were in love. She looked at him as if attaching skate wheels was the most tremendous feat a man could accomplish.

Sally took Nat's hand and they glided onto the roller rink. He held her around the waist as they moved to a skater's waltz played by a small band seated on a platform above the rink. She had on a blue cotton summer dress, the ankle-length skirt cut wide so that she could skate, and a wide-brimmed straw hat, secured tightly with hatpins, to protect her from the intense sun.

All around them couples rolled sedately as boys dashed in and out, just barely avoiding upsetting the other skaters. "Only a Dream," went the music, and iron skates grated against the stone floor as the skaters swirled by in a stream of bright colors, chatter, and laughter. At times there was a crash and cries as someone, usually one of the unruly boys, fell.

Beyond the palings of the wrought iron fence, aspens and tall cottonwoods danced in the light breeze, and strollers along the park's paths enjoyed the warm June afternoon. Overhead, a wedge of honking geese headed for the pond.

Nat pulled Sally closer, his brown eyes warm with smiles. She felt as if she were flying, no longer a human being but a bird, skimming through the air. They crossed hands and the waltz sent them around and around. Then the music died down for a short break.

"Let's get a drink." Nat pulled her toward the edge of the rink.

Sally wanted to protest that she was enjoying the skating and not ready for a drink.

But when Nat said drink, that was what they would have, and they proceeded to a lemonade stand. He was, as some would put it, masterful.

Sally thought he was just plain bossy. But she expected that was the way boys were.

She looked at him with smiling eyes just above the rim of her lemonade glass, a gesture she had borrowed from a sarsaparilla ad, with a girl in a sailor blouse—on a boat—looking dreamily over a glass of sarsaparilla at a handsome man.

"My father's made me a manager at the firm," said Nat. He always called his father's freight business "the firm."

"How wonderful!" Sally exclaimed. "What are your duties?"

"I schedule the wagons going out."

She batted her eyes, hoping she didn't look ridiculous. Eye batters usually had long black lashes, not stubby blonde ones. "That sounds so interesting. Such a responsibility." She had to remember their dialogue so that she could go over it later with Carrie. Maybe it was overdone.

Nat didn't think so. He beamed.

Sally smiled winningly. Carrie and Simon came whirling past them and she waved, delicately.

"What about college?" she asked, forgetting to keep her voice milk chocolate sweet and admiring.

"I've had enough," said Nat. "Waste of time. All that literature and poetry and French. A man needs to know how to keep a ledger and to satisfy customers."

"Oh?" said Sally, instead of nodding agreeably.

Hanging between them were the unsaid words. Her brothers were going to college, studying professions.

Nat had a vaguely annoyed look on his face. She'd messed up again. And she couldn't think of a thing to say that would make it all right.

"C'mon," she pulled his hand. "Let's skate. You're such a wonderful skater, you make me feel as if I'm flying."

His face became sunny again and he drew her out on the rink with a flourish.

All of this catering to him was beginning to give her a headache. Why does a woman have to spend her whole life worrying about what she says to a man, keeping him in a good mood, she wondered, as she snuggled close and they skated, endlessly, in a circle. After a while it stopped being fun and became boring.

Finally Simon skated over and said that he and Carrie had had enough. The two couples drove home in Nat's elegant open phaeton with two high-stepping black horses. In the back seat, Carrie and Simon held hands. Nat pointed with his whip to a

building his father owned. The wood was unpaint-
ed and Sally noticed cardboard over broken glass.

"Your father needs to do quite a lot of fixing,"
she said, and then snapped her mouth shut.
Tactless, tactless!

Nat laughed. "That's why he bought the building cheap. He doesn't have to fix it up much. The
people who live there are just riffraff."

A child wearing just a dirty undershirt was playing in the mud in front of the building and a scruffy-
looking lean dog came sniffing around. Sally wondered what made people into riffraff. Poverty? She
looked at Nat, so handsome beside her handling
the reins and she longed to speak to him about
poverty and why people were poor and how they
could be helped. And she knew that it would be
like speaking to him in a strange language.

There was a clear stretch ahead in the traffic.
Nat leaned forward and, with glistening eyes,
lashed the horses and sent them galloping. Carrie
squealed and Sally held onto her hat.

As buildings and trees went by in a blur, Sally had
a fleeting glimpse of a newsboy standing in front of
Joslin's. Nat's excited laugh and Carrie's giggling
yell faded in the background as Sally's eyes were
drawn to the newsboy, shouting "Tribune, get your
Tribune here."

Clogged traffic forced Nat to slow the horses
down. Sally stared at the boy. There were newsboys all over town but she knew who he was—
Daniel, the dirty boy Aunt Frank had brought to the

confirmation party. He wasn't dirty now. He seemed to have had a haircut and he was wearing new pants.

Daniel looked up and he saw her and, boldly, he smiled and raised a newspaper in greeting. She raised her hand and waved, not delicately, but vigorously.

"Who's that?" Nat demanded.

"Why, it's the boy whose mother collapsed. Don't you remember? Mrs. Jacobs brought him to Sally's house the day of the confirmation party," said Carrie.

"And he waved?" Nat gave the horses a smart crack of the whip and they dashed through a hole in the traffic, almost upsetting a wagonload of rickety furniture. The driver shouted words that Sally had never heard. Nat thumbed his nose at him.

"That was vulgar," scolded Sally.

"Who are you to talk about vulgar?" he replied meanly. "I saw you wave at that filthy newsboy. Talk of arrogance, he had some nerve to wave at us. These people are swarming all over town and they don't know their place."

"He wasn't waving at *you*," Sally muttered.

"What did you say?" he said sharply.

"Never mind," she subsided. This argument had become painful.

"I don't like it when you mumble," said Nat. "Sally, you must learn to speak clearly. Perhaps next year you can study elocution in school."

"Looks like Mama has a houseful," remarked Simon as they reached the Gottesman house. Carriages were lined up all along the front of the house.

"It's the Ladies' Sewing Circle from the temple," said Sally.

"I'm not going in there," Simon declared. "I'll just hide out in Carrie's house."

Nat walked Sally to the door. "Look Sally, I really like you. I mean, if I yelled at you I hope I didn't make you mad. It's just that that fresh newsboy got me riled. Now don't you go being friendly to that kind. You give them a hand and they'll take an arm. Promise, Sally?"

"It'll be all right," she said.

"Good. I want to spend a lot of time with you this summer. I don't work all the time, you know," he laughed. "After all, I'm the boss's son."

"Fine," said Sally quickly. He bent over as if to kiss her but she drew away and pretended she didn't see. "Thanks for the nice afternoon."

He shrugged, then turned and marched down the steps and the walk to his carriage.

The sound of talk and laughter and the smell of coffee and cakes drew her to the parlor, where the sewing ladies were industriously making baby garments for the poor. To keep them amused, Clara Gottesman read from a newspaper, with mock solemnity. "A glass bedstead has been produced in England and exhibited in London."

"Whatever for?" giggled Minna Schayer.

"Slippin' and slidin' all over the bed!" exclaimed Eva Koenigsberg.

"Oh, Eva, you're wicked," exclaimed Mrs. Schayer, and the women slapped their knees. Lily Wisebart, Frances Jacobs' sister-in-law, gave a little squeal. "Now I've stuck myself with a needle."

Clara noticed Sally standing at the archway leading from the hall. "Hello, sweetie, you know all of the ladies, don't you?"

Sally smiled. She'd known them since babyhood.

"Do you have time to do some sewing? We promised Frankie we'd finish this load of baby garments for her to take tomorrow to the families who live in Tent City."

Sally picked up a pile of precut baby shirts and a needle and white thread. Carefully, with tiny stitches, as she had been taught, she began to sew up a seam. The women nodded with approval. Sally might be one of those modern girls, running off with boys unchaperoned, but she still had her housewifely training.

"Here's one," said Clara, earnestly peering at the newspaper. "Now listen, ladies. This is not funny. 'The Senate of Colorado evidently considers woman as a creature to be petted and caressed, fondled and taken care of and not fitted to cope in the struggles of life like a man. The honorable body of honorable gentlemen are gallant, courteous and brave, but they do not believe that lovely women will make good public notaries. Senator Elkins says he voted against a petition to allow women to become notaries because he did not think that woman should be encouraged in swearing, and, further, that as a swearer she is never much of a success'."

"Oh shoot," exclaimed Frances Jacobs. "In Central City in the old days I heard enough to turn you blue. Not to mention the choice language used by the men we met in the oxcarts and flatboats when I traveled to Denver as a bride."

"Anyway, a notary doesn't cuss," said Ida Kohn, whose husband was in the legislature. "They just say 'Do you solemnly swear that you are such and such a person and the statements made in this document are true?' I told my husband George that, and I made him promise that he would vote for the petition."

Clara stabbed a needle into a baby blanket as if it were an offending man. "The men make up these things to keep women down. They think we're going to take away their jobs or something."

"Women have jobs," said Frances sarcastically. "Women down in the tents have jobs. They're widows or else their men have run off to the mines and never come back. They work for two dollars and fifty cents a week cleaning or doing other menial jobs, and they're supposed to support families on that."

"Women need better education," suggested Ida Kohn. "If they have more skills, they can get better jobs."

"We *must* have the vote," said Clara firmly. "If the politicians know women won't vote for them they won't pass such wicked legislation. I don't know what's the matter with the women of Colorado. Susan Anthony and Carrie Chapman Catt and Lucy Stone came all the way from New York to help us when the State Constitution was written in 1877. But what did we get?"

"We got the right to vote in school elections," said Mrs. Ellie Appel mildly.

"Oh, hip hip hooray," said Clara, glaring at Frances Jacobs.

Frances spread her hands. "Don't blame Abraham. He was on the Constitution committee but he couldn't buck those other women-hating cavemen. How are we doing on the sewing?" She gathered up the load of clothes into her ever-present basket. "I have some more things I must bring down to the tents . . . Sally, do you think you can give me a hand tomorrow?"

"Of course," said Sally. "School's out for the summer."

As Sally climbed into the small one-horse buggy early the next morning, Frances nodded in approval. "I'm glad you had enough sense to wear something simple. We don't want to show off to the people we're going to see . . . you know, the rich ladies coming to aid the downtrodden."

Sally laughed. That was exactly the way some

people she knew viewed charity . . . us and poor them. She shifted to get out of the way of a bundle.

"Just throw those things up on the back," said Frances. "Sally, do you know the meaning of the Hebrew word, *tzedakah*?"

"Of course. Charity."

"Wrong again," Frances exclaimed. "There is no word for charity in Hebrew. *Tzedakah* means to do the right thing. I am my brother's or my sister's keeper. Someone may be in need today. Tomorrow may be my turn."

Sally considered that as the horse clip-clopped down toward the Platte River. If you put it that way, it made it easier to meet the people who were going to get the clothes. She'd been nervous about that. Did you pity them? Or pretend that everything was wonderful? No, you thought, "Sister, you're having hard times. I'm helping you and if I have hard times I hope someone will help me."

The buggy stopped at the edge of the river and Frances hitched the horse to a tree. Picking up their skirts, Sally and Frances walked toward what seemed to be piles of old lumber. As they neared Tent City, Sally noticed that it was a crude village with a narrow muddy lane along which tattered tents and crazily built shacks made of slapped-together boards and flattened tin cans crowded one upon the other.

Mangy dogs slunk among piles of garbage. There was a stench of outhouses. Suddenly Sally shrieked, "Aunt Frank, a rat!" as the rodent scurried under a gap and into a house.

Frances regarded the disappearing rat with disinterest. "Place is full of rats. And every other kind of running and crawling creature you can find. Including people," she added grimly.

"But the children," cried Sally. The lane was full of children in diapers, or torn pinafores or patched pants, running, yelling, throwing stones. There was no evidence of toys or go-carts such as she and her brothers used to play with.

"The children get bitten by rats. Sometimes, rats climb over the babies in their cribs."

A tiny girl with flaxen curls tugged at Frances' skirt. She looked up shyly, her thumb in her mouth.

"Hello, Susie," said Frances. "Do you want some candy?" As Susie looked up with intent round blue eyes, Frances searched through one of her bags. "I thought I had some." The dirty little face puckered with worry. "Ah," said Frances, "here it is." She held up a stick of candy and the little girl reached.

"Say please," said Frances.

"Pleeese," parroted the little girl.

Frances handed her the candy. "Now," she said holding up a finger. "What do we say?"

"Thank you," piped the little voice.

"Smart little girl. You remember. Now take this cake of tar soap home to Mama and tell her to wash your face." Frances handed the child a bar of her tar soap.

As the little girl skipped off, sucking on the candy, Frances reflected, "Manners, you think, are a luxury when people have no food. Not at all. They may need emergency help now, but they also must learn to get along in the world."

Frances knocked on the door of one of the ramshackle houses. It was opened by a tired-looking young woman with stringy hair and exhausted dark-circled gray eyes, wearing a torn faded gingham house dress that might once have been blue. Beyond her, in the dim light of the one-room shack, Sally saw a boy of about seven sitting at a homemade table munching on a piece of bread and jam. Fretful cries came from a box in the corner, where a baby lay in a nest of rags.

"Mrs. Ryan, I'm Frances Jacobs from the Ladies' Relief Society." This was a non-sectarian organization Frances had formed when the city's needs became too great to be met by the Hebrew Benevolent Ladies Aid Society alone. "We hear that you are in need."

Mrs. Ryan moved aside and Frances stepped briskly into the house, timidly followed by Sally.

Flustered, Mrs. Ryan tried to find them chairs, shooing her son off the one he was sitting on and finally dragging out a small footstool for Sally. "I'm sorry, the place is a mess." Nervously she smoothed her apron and touched her hair. "There's mud all around," she finished lamely.

"That's all right." Frances gave Mrs. Ryan one of her warm wonderful smiles. "We're not company.

This is my assistant, Sally Gottesman. You might remember her father, Dr. Gottesman."

"Ah, a blessed man," said Mrs. Ryan in a soft brogue. "He helped Mrs. Mitchell down the street. Saved her life."

The boy, still chewing on what seemed to be stale bread, had positioned himself in front of them, staring. He had an impudent little pointed chin. Sally had the feeling he could be a mischief when he wasn't overawed.

"This here's Timothy, Timothy Junior," Mrs. Ryan sighed. "Go outside in the air and play, Timmy."

Bobbing his head at the visitors, Timmy ran out the door.

"My man left me," said Mrs. Ryan tiredly. "We come all the way from Pennsylvania in a wagon. He said he was going to find gold and he told me not to worry, he'd be back. But he went off to the mines and I never saw him again. I guess he didn't find any gold and was ashamed to come back empty-handed." She lifted her apron in a helpless gesture as tears suddenly rolled down her cheeks.

"It's very sad," agreed Frances, finding a clean handkerchief for the woman. "But we're here to see that you're not alone . . . Mrs. Ryan."

"Bridie," the woman sniffed her first name and blew her nose into the handkerchief.

"Now," said Frances once more all business. "Let's determine your needs. You have a young baby, I see."

Bridie smiled and went to the box and lifted out the baby. Red-faced, the infant screwed up her mouth and let out a wail and her tiny fingers grabbed at her mother.

"Aaah," said Frances. "Such a fine young . . . girl is it? And her name?"

"Maggie—that is, Margaret, for me mother, back in Ireland," said Bridie. She held the wailing baby awkwardly. "Hush," she pleaded, but the child continued to cry.

Frances laughed. "Don't be modest, Bridie. We're all women here. Nurse your baby."

Bridie opened her blouse and the baby began to suck contentedly. "You'll need some nourishing food so your milk will be good for the baby. And the boy needs good food too. A basket will be delivered to you every week until you get on your feet. And we've brought some things from the women of Temple Emanuel, made by their own hands, to give your little one a good start."

Bridie examined the tiny garments with admiration. "Now aren't they beautiful! Such sewing. Little stitches like me sainted mother taught me. The blessed women. Thank them for me."

"I'll do that," Frances promised. "Now Bridie, don't you be afraid. You have friends in this city. You are not alone. One more thing," and she brought out two bars of tar soap. "Here's some soap to keep the children clean."

"Ah, yes," Bridie smiled proudly. "I keep my

young ones tidy, or at least I try to." With the baby still at her breast, she walked them to the door. "May the saints bless you both," she said.

"And you," laughed Frances, quoting an Irish proverb. "May the wind always be at your back."

They went to other houses and tents, distributing necessities and children's clothing and always, Frances gave a bit more, a message of hope.

As they picked their way through the mud back to the buggy, Sally said, "Is there something I can do to help? It seems wicked for me, almost sixteen, to just idle away the summer months."

"You like children, don't you?" Frances asked.

"I do. Very much."

"Very well. I shall speak to Miss Griswold, who runs our little kindergarten over in West Colfax. It's a school we started like the ones I saw in San Francisco. Gives the little ones a good start before they go to public school and frees the mothers to go out and earn some money, little as that is."

Chapter 6

Sally went down to Joslin's Department Store early on Saturday morning to buy a new shirtwaist, one that would be proper when teaching small children. Something plain, definitely washable. Probably white. She settled on a blouse with a small ruffled collar, modest but not too prim.

Leaving the store, she happened to run into Daniel. Actually, she didn't exactly run into him. He had moved his newspaper selling spot more toward the corner and she had to saunter down the block, looking into shop windows, before she saw him.

"Why . . ." she said in her most gracious, surprised voice, twirling a pretty pink parasol she'd brought along just for this purpose. "It's, uh,

Daniel. You came with Mrs. Jacobs to our house during the confirmation party. So sorry to hear about your mother. And how is your dear mother?"

"Sick," he said briefly. "Very sick."

He was staring at her. He had the most remarkable eyes she'd ever seen, large and green, with brown flecks which seemed to change to blue flecks according to the light. They were like corridors of endless color, leading deeply into wonderful fantasies of thought. There was something else . . . little sparks of light. Humor. Sally had the uneasy feeling he was laughing at her.

"Rabinowitz," he said very distinctly. "Daniel Rabinowitz."

As if hypnotized, Sally repeated, "Daniel Rabinowitz."

He smiled, the way one would at a bright child. There was a curl to his mouth as if he found the world, in its folly, amusing. He was not a handsome fellow, she decided. His face was too bony, his nose too large. He was not very tall. He had nice hair, though, the color of mahogany. It was thick and straight and flopped over his forehead. She had the insane desire to smooth it back.

"Sarah Gottesman," he announced, bringing forth from his pocket a wrinkled copy of the newspaper article reporting on the Temple Emanuel confirmation. He ran a long square-nailed finger down the list of names of the confirmands until he came to hers. It was underlined.

Excitement, like little caterpillars, moved in her stomach. So she had not imagined it! He really had stared at her that afternoon when Aunt Frank brought him to the house. And it was to her that he had waved when she went by in Nat's buggy.

She laughed. "My name's Sarah, but everyone calls me Sally."

"Sally," he repeated. "*Shayne maydel.*"

She knew enough German to understand his Yiddish. Pretty girl! Nat was right. Daniel certainly didn't know his place. In fact, he didn't know he had a place.

She blushed. "Thank you." Then she pointed at him. "Handsome."

He looked puzzled.

"*Shayne*," she said. "You."

He made a face. "No!"

"Your eyes." She seemed to be under a spell, saying such things to a boy she hardly knew. "*Shayne.*"

"Ha, ha," he laughed. "*Shayne eugen.*" He took out a tattered book, with ENGLISH GRAMMAR printed in big letters on its cover, and a small dictionary. "I learn much English. My boss, Mr. Eugene Field, Tribune editor, teach me. I learn English. I talk to you. Tell you many things."

He was leaning toward her as if he were going to touch her, but he only touched her with his eyes, looking up and down.

"Do you like working for Mr. Field?"

"Yes. Funny man. Always laugh. Good man.

Good to newsboys." He pointed to his pants. "Give me new pants. Good friend."

"Mr. Field is a writer. He wrote a sad poem, 'Little Boy Blue,' that made everyone cry. And he plays jokes. Once a famous writer, Oscar Wilde, was coming to Denver for a public appearance but he was delayed. Mr. Field put on a wig and funny clothes and pretended he was Oscar Wilde. He rode all through the city and people cheered him."

While she spoke, Daniel looked at her intently. He didn't seem to understand all her words, but she was aware of his mind, like an efficient machine, capturing the English words and making them his own.

"Did you find a place to live?" she asked.

"Yes, nice room in West Colfax. With a bathtub." He moved his shoulders a little, embarrassed, and she wondered if he was ashamed at the memory of how he looked when Frances brought him to the Gottesmans' home during the party. "I vash me and vash clothes."

"I can bathe and wash my clothes," she corrected.

He stepped back with a look of shock, pointing at her. "You are going to bathe and vash your clothes in my bathtub?"

Sally sputtered with laughter. "You're horrible!"

Quickly he consulted his dictionary. "'Horrible: frightening, causing horror.'" He came at her with his teeth bared and his fingers curved into claws.

"Aaargh, I horrible. I get you!"

A passing policeman stopped. "Is this fellow bothering you, young lady?"

"Yes, officer," she said sweetly. "He's turning into a werewolf."

The policeman shook his head in confusion, gave Jacob a warning glance, and moved on.

"Vhat is werewolf?" asked Jacob.

"A half-man, half-wolf. He eats people, I think."

"Ahhh . . . ." He stroked an imaginary beard. "It is written in the holy books that beautiful girls should always be eaten by werewolfs. Only *kosher* girls, of course."

A man came to buy a newspaper and Daniel expertly gave him change.

"I'm interfering with your work," said Sally.

"In-ter-fer-ing," repeated Daniel, filing the word away in his mind.

"Bothering," she explained.

Swiftly, he consulted his dictionary. "'Bothering: annoying, troubling'" He thumbed some more. "'Annoying: pestering, irritating."

"You don't interfere, bother, pester, irritate. When you here, I happy."

As his eyes, full of light, fixed on her, she realized with shock, that this strange newsboy had fallen in love with her. Instantly. The moment he'd seen her.

People didn't do that.

But there it was.

It was a strange and enormous thing and it made

her feel all shaky inside. Her family loved her and that was comfortable. Nat seemed to like her, but he was more interested in stealing kisses and touching her than caring about her.

But in one second Daniel's complicated, wonderful green eyes shone upon her and, without being told, loved everything about her, every secret thought, every fault. Although it would hardly be proper here on a street corner, Sally felt embraced, not touched for a boy's pleasure, but protected and enclosed. And she wanted to embrace Daniel too, to close the circle. She wondered if he saw that in her eyes. He must have, for he was smiling.

Nervously, she stepped back. "I have to go home now," she stammered. She touched him on the shoulder and said, "Be happy," and turned and swiftly walked away.

"Good by, *shayne maydel* Sally Gottesman," he called after her. "I will see you many times."

On the way home in the horsecar, she relived the encounter, chuckling a little, until she realized that the lady seated next to her, a pudgy woman with many bundles tied with string, was staring at her.

Primly, she folded her hands in her lap and glanced out the window. A book she'd recently read, *The Little Minister*, by James M. Barrie, came to mind. It was about a young minister who fell in love with a Gypsy girl named Babbie. How could he introduce her to his congregation?

Suppose she showed up at a temple dance with Daniel, with his newsboy cap and broken English. She shuddered at the thought.

And yet, the brief time on the street corner with him had been more fun than a whole afternoon roller skating with Nat.

Dr. Gottesman insisted on driving Sally to the kindergarten where she was to teach. "West Colfax is no place for a young lady to go alone," he declared.

They drove down Hartman Avenue (later to be called Colfax Avenue), past the hill where the state capitol was to be built, past impressive mansions, until they came to the Platte River. When they crossed the river, the street name changed to Golden Avenue, the heart of the settlement of West Colfax. Immigrants had arrived, first in a trickle by wagon and then, when railroads were built, in a torrent. They came for gold, to build a better life, many of them seeking health in the dry Colorado air.

After the first Russian pogroms in 1881, Jews came to Denver from the East European Pale of Settlement in Russia and Poland, escaping from Tsarist tyranny. Some were the remnants of failed Colorado agricultural experiments, interested in a socialist life rather than in religion.

A small number were *Hasidim*, bearded men wearing hats and fringed garments under their jackets and followed by meek wives in long-sleeved dresses and kerchiefs over their wigs, and always, by children. But most were ordinary folk from the small shtetls who refused to live under the painful restrictions of their native lands where good education was almost impossible, many occupations forbidden, and freedom to live wherever they wanted denied.

Small, shabby but neat wooden houses lined the crowded street and dingy shops displayed signs in English and Yiddish. Peddlers urged undernourished horses on the way to sell their wares in outlying districts. Dogs barked and children yelled. Small boys darted among the wagons. Food vendors called out their wares.

As the doctor's horse and buggy made their way past wagons and carts, occasionally someone tipped his hat respectfully—Dr. Gottesman's buggy was well known. "Here it is," he said, somehow maneuvering the horse and buggy into a vacant space next to a hitching post.

Anxiously, to make sure this was a place where he could safely leave his daughter, Dr. Gottesman escorted Sally into the school. The small building had recently been painted and seemed reasonably clean. They walked past several brightly decorated rooms, some with tiny children sleeping on mats or in cribs, others with older youngsters playing and talking. It was peaceful, a building filled with the music of little voices, and occasionally the sound of a piano and singing. He met Miss Emily Griswold, the director, a pleasant woman in her thirties, with neat brown hair drawn back into a bun. Reassured, the doctor left, telling Sally he would return in the afternoon to pick her up.

Miss Griswold found a place in her cluttered office for Sally to sit.

"I understand that you play the piano," she said.

"Yes. My mother was a music teacher. She taught me." Sally did not mention the battles Clara had fought to make her practice. But she could play tolerably, at least well enough to accompany children's songs.

"Good. I'm going to put you with the older children. We need someone there. They're five years old, and very, uh, lively. Most of them come from deprived backgrounds. They have not had pretty picture books read to them or doting parents teaching them their colors. In fact, some of them barely know English. But I am sure you will do fine."

She led the way to a classroom, where fifteen children, seated at low tables, were earnestly coloring under the watchful eye of a pretty redheaded young woman. "This is Elsie O'Neil," Miss Griswold said. "Elsie's been substituting here since this group's teacher went back east for a vacation.

"Elsie, this is Sally Gottesman. She'll be taking the class for the rest of the summer. Please tell her where everything is, and then you can go back to the babies. You're needed there."

Elsie explained about the toy closet and the art closet and showed Sally a music book of children's games. "I guess you know most of these," she said.

"'Ring Around the Rosy' does sound a little familiar," Sally laughed. She was conscious of the children's eyes staring at her, but they were all very quiet and, in fact, rather solemn. "You bring them in to the lunch room at noon," Elsie told her. "They always have a good hot lunch; for many of them it's their only good meal of the day."

While she was speaking, a grandmotherly-looking woman with a round rosy face and a fringe of white hair came in. "Hello, Mrs. Kobey," said Elsie. "This is Sally Gottesman, our new teacher. Mary Kobey is the neighborhood midwife. She keeps track of her babies, makes sure they stay healthy."

Mrs. Kobey gave Sally a warm smile. "I come to watch Aaron." She spoke with a Yiddish accent. "His little *feisele* were not right and they had to put them in a cast. I want to see him walk." She went over to a small boy. "Get up and valk for Grandma Kobey." Obediently, Aaron got up and walked around the table.

"Beautiful!" she exclaimed. "Just for that, you get a lemon drop." Reaching into an enormous black leather reticule, she brought forth a candy which the little boy quickly popped into his mouth.

Looking around, Mrs. Kobey slapped her cheeks with her hands. "There are more children! I did not know. Oh my, do I have any more lemon drops?" The children laughed. They knew Grandma Kobey was joking. "Ahah!" She brought out a paper sack and handed lemon drops to all the children.

"Good-by," she called. "Miss Sally, have a good time with the children."

"I'm going to leave you now too," said Elsie. "Will you be all right?"

"Of course," said Sally. But when she was alone with the children, all staring at her with a "what next?" expression, she had a feeling of panic. What next, indeed?

She walked around, admiring their coloring work. A little boy got up and went over to the toy trains.

"Are you supposed to be doing that?" asked Sally, puzzled. "I thought this was coloring time."

The boy looked at her uncertainly and went on playing with the trains. Suddenly, all the boys jumped up and ran for toys.

"Teacher, teacher," said a little girl. "I have to go potty."

"Where is it?" Sally looked around. Maybe this old building didn't have indoor plumbing. It did, pointed out to her by a prim little girl named Monica. Sally took little Esther to the bathroom and made sure she washed her hands. The bathroom had been well supplied with Frances Jacobs' tar soap.

When Sally returned to the classroom, she said amiably to the little girls, "Let's pick up the crayons" but they swished by her to the doll corner. Doggedly, Sally gathered up all the crayons and put them into a box. The atmosphere in the room was becoming completely chaotic.

Two boys got into a fight over a toy wagon. Their faces red, they screamed at each other in Yiddish. While Sally was trying to separate them, a heavyset boy named Pedro hit one of the little girls, who promptly sat on the floor and screamed. Sally left the battling boys and ran over to the little girl, picking her up and examining her to make sure she wasn't injured.

"You're a bad boy!" she scolded Pedro, who cocked his head and said in Spanish, "*No se* (I don't understand)."

Standing in the middle of the room, Sally felt as if she were in the middle of a lake in a boat without a rudder or oars. Desperately, she ran to the piano. "We are going to sing songs, children." She started playing "Jack and Jill Went Up the Hill."

Several little girls and one blue-eyed boy named William came and sat cross-legged near the piano and obediently sang, but the other children were too busy. Several had discovered a new game, in which one boy sat on a chair and another child pushed him around the room. Four boys were busy throwing building blocks at each other, faster and faster, and then all over the room, chortling with glee.

Suddenly, the door to the hallway opened. Miss Griswold stood there, perfectly silent, glaring.

Like magic, all the children stopped what they

were doing and rushed to their seats, their hands clasped in front of them on the tables. "Heads down," said Miss Griswold in a hard voice. Fifteen heads went down on the tables.

Miss Griswold then addressed Sally, her voice no longer friendly. "Do you think you can manage to get them to the lunch room? It's after twelve."

Stricken, Sally nodded yes. She had forgotten all about lunch.

Somehow, she shepherded the children down the corridor to the lunch room. Elsie O'Neil appeared and helped her keep them in some kind of order and then returned to the classroom with Sally after lunch and helped her lay out the mats for the children to sleep on. Exhausted from all the excitement, the children soon drowsed off, and Elsie tiptoed out, whispering, "When they wake up, they can go outside."

The afternoon passed. The children rested and so did Sally. Later, outdoors in the little yard, it didn't matter how much they ran and yelled. There was a problem with throwing sand in the sandbox, and Esther got sand in her eye and Sally had to take her inside to have it washed out. Finally the endless day ended and the mothers came for their children.

Miss Griswold called Sally into her office. "The children were out of control," she said severely.

"I know," Sally mumbled.

"We can't have this. I don't know what Mrs. Jacobs was thinking about, sending such an inexperienced person. I know you're a volunteer, but we still must have order."

"They wouldn't listen," Sally burst out, holding back tears. She would not cry. She would not cry. If she couldn't control the children, at least she could control herself.

"Well," sighed Miss Griswold, "We are desperate to keep that class covered. Come back tomorrow and we'll give you another chance."

Outside, sitting on the stone stoop waiting for her father, Sally finally burst into sobs.

"And so, little Miss Sally, what is the trouble?" Mrs. Kobey stood before her, her brown eyes behind silver-rimmed spectacles warm with concern.

"The children don't like me. I like the children, but they don't care. They can see that I'm a great stupid girl and I don't know what to do."

"Now, now, listen to Grandma." Mrs. Kobey put a hand on Sally's arm. "How would you know?" she shrugged. "Me, I know because I raised mine own children, mine grandchildren. Believe me, they gave me plenty grief. See, these *kinder*, they come from mixed-up homes. Nobody ever tells them what to do. You don't ask them—Tell! You don't yell. You don't hit.

"You just tell them, but you make it simple, one child at a time. 'Time to line up, Johnny, Betty . . .' One child after another. 'Time to come to sing. Johnny, Betty . . .' they come. One child you can do. A whole class, no. They don't hear.

"And when there's funny business, you send the child to the corner. Make him sit there while something good is going on. They hate that, to miss something. If they promise to be good, you let them come back."

Mrs. Kobey tilted Sally's chin up and looked at her with her warm, kind eyes. "Oh, such a beautiful girl. The children will love you. Such a beautiful smart teacher. But you got to let them know you're the boss."

Dr. Gottesman's buggy pulled up in front of the building. He raised his buggy whip in greeting. "Hello, Mary."

"Hello, Doctor," called Mrs. Kobey, and hurried back along the sidewalk, on the way to her many errands of mercy.

"Best doctor in town, that midwife," commented Sally's father. "How did it go?"

"All right." Sally said. "Actually," she amended, "It was pretty awful. The children didn't behave and the principal blamed me. But Mrs. Kobey gave me some advice. Tomorrow, I'll see if it works."

Her father looked at her and nodded with satisfaction. "Good. Remember, Gottesmans are never quitters."

Chapter 7

Sally could not believe that fifteen wild five-year-olds could be tamed by Mary Kobey's simple suggestions, but she had nothing to lose. The next day, she made sure to get to school before the children arrived. With a list of their names in hand, she stood at the classroom door and greeted each one and told the child to sit quietly at a table until everyone arrived. Amazingly, Mrs. Kobey's idea worked. Perhaps a mob of children did not obey, but one child did. . . . After all, the children realized that she was bigger, and smarter.

This didn't follow when it came to the mothers. Many of them only a few years older than herself, they were a suspicious group. Yesterday, the children had gone home with tales of how they'd had "fun" and how the new teacher didn't seem to care.

Most of the mothers looked shabby, even down-right bedraggled. Some of them spoke no English. But their children were precious to them. They held on to them like valuable packages, afraid to leave them with a teacher who "didn't care." Miss Griswold finally appeared, reassuring them. "Miss Gottesman is our new teacher. If she has any problems, I'll be right here to help out."

She smiled archly at Sally, who felt her heart sink down to her new high-button shoes. Her look seemed to say Miss Gottesman is an idiot, but she wouldn't let her harm the children too much.

When the mothers reluctantly left their children, and Miss Griswold, with another of her icy smiles, went back to her office, Sally faced her class once again.

The class. It wasn't just a class. These were fifteen different people. First of all, she needed to memorize all their names.

She seated herself in front of them, modestly spreading her long black skirt and smoothing her hair, which she had pinned up into a bun in back of her head. A little boy started to get up and run to the toy corner. But Sally wasn't taken by surprise this time. "No!" she said firmly. Hastily, the boy sat down. His friends, who had been watching to see what would happen, changed their minds about running off too.

"My name is Miss Gottesman," she told them,

although they probably knew that. "Let me hear you say that." Then she remembered what Mary had told her. "One at a time."

As she pointed to each child, he or she made a great effort to say her name correctly, and Sally realized something. They were competitive; they liked to show off in front of one another. "Very, very good," she said to each one, even if they got it wrong. Mustn't let them look foolish in front of others. It had hurt her to feel stupid yesterday. How much more would it hurt a child?

Mentally, she created Sally's Rule Number One: Each child is important. Rule Number Two: Each child is valuable.

When they had all learned her name, she had them repeat their own names . . . she looked hard at their faces as they spoke so that she would remember the names. Then she had the children tell about their families. As each one spoke she registered things about the child; how he spoke English, whether she was shy or frightened, if he was immature.

This was beginning to get interesting. It was like reading fifteen different books, each with its own plot.

Painstakingly, very slowly, she moved through the day, bringing the children one by one into groups for singing and for coloring, and meanwhile watching, watching, for any break in discipline. Monica and Pedro each spent some time in the corner for unruly behavior and the other children watched them out of the corners of their eyes.

The next day, instead of calling the children into groups individually, she gave them colored paper and divided them into teams. "Let's see which team is the quietest and they can be first in line for lunch." Eagerly the teams competed, stifling misbehaving members.

Sally had learned something—the children were not only competitive individually, but competitive in groups, and that made things go much faster. Besides, they were learning their colors.

Sally stared at the children, now diligently coloring. What was really going on here? She resolved to learn all about each child and how he or she fitted into the group. And suddenly, she stopped thinking about herself and how well she was controlling the children and what Miss Griswold and the mothers thought of her. This was a very fascinating game! It was not only about the children and their personalities but also about how learning was going on.

She became aware of what she was doing and how each activity taught something. Singing and chanting games were for language. Stories were for listening. Coloring and cutouts were for learning to use hands and fingers. A few children were able to scrawl their names, their first writing.

The group had a structure—strong people who told the others what to do . . . weak people, like little William, who were always victims. That's the way classes were. Her own classes, even her confirmation class, was that way.

Monica and Pedro were leaders, sometimes bullying the others. But she could use them. If she got them to start an activity, the others followed.

One day Sally decided to teach the children the names of the parts of the body. She spread out a big piece of paper on the floor and asked William to lie down on it. With much giggling from William, she traced the outline of his body on the paper and then hung the paper on the wall, labeled in big letters "WILLIAM."

William, immensely pleased, was now a celebrity! Sally noticed that the children played more with him outside.

As Sally got more and more involved, she began to see other patterns. Certain children, especially girls, wanted to sit together, and they worked better when she let them although there was much more chatter. Then there were children who didn't seem to be in a group. Sally tried them out with one group after another until she found one that accepted them.

Coming from crowded, disordered homes, many of the children were not used to having anyone listen to them, especially now that English was becoming their natural language, sometimes different from the family tongue. With the class now functioning smoothly, Sally found the time to sit on a little chair next to each child and talk about the picture he'd drawn, what he liked to do most, and once in a while about things that made him or her unhappy. Sometimes these talks gave her ideas about what was going on at the child's home but she kept her mouth shut. She'd learned the first day that children are little town criers and whatever you say is repeated.

She fell in love with teaching. Throughout the hot summer she drove eagerly with her father to West Colfax and reluctantly gave the children back to their mothers at the end of the day. Some of the mothers thanked her and shyly handed her little gifts, like a box of home-made cookies. Even Miss Griswold, relieved that there was no more trouble, grudgingly told her to "keep up the good work."

"It's as if a door opened for me," she chattered to her father one afternoon when they were driving home. "All my life I've done things because someone told me to do it. But this . . . I have to figure everything out myself. It's so exciting."

"We all need to succeed at something," her father remarked. "So now you're growing up. Sixteen next month. And who will you invite to your party?"

Annoyed, Sally turned her head away, staring at the passing traffic. Here she was talking about something important, about herself, and all Papa could think about was a party. That's how he thought of her—as an ornament you dress up in a party dress.

"Are you angry with me?" he asked, surprised.

"No," she said sulkily.

"So why don't you answer me? Whom are you inviting to your party?"

She shrugged. "Carrie, the brothers, Lena Wald."

"And Nat," he said encouragingly.

"And Nat. He's taken me to picnics and dancing and once to the theater. I guess I owe him something."

"You don't sound very enthusiastic. I thought you liked Nat?"

"He's all right," she said uneasily.

Abstractedly, Dr. Gottesman let the horses find their own pace. "You are, of course, too young to think seriously of any young man, But soon, Sally, the right man will come along for you. Remember, your mother was married at eighteen. It is proper for a woman to marry young. When girls are, well, too picky, things seem to pass them by. The best men are taken by less particular girls. And then we have the sad spectacle of spinsters, of old-maid school teachers."

"I don't think teachers are sad. Teaching is very exciting." He hadn't listened to a word she told him!

"Of course. And teaching school is a nice occupation for a little while. But a girl must marry and have a home. Do you understand me?"

"Certainly. You want me to marry Nat Wald."

"That's ridiculous." He became very agitated. Sally wondered if her mother had put him up to this conversation.   "You're much too young to think of anyone seriously. It's just that your mother and I . . ." So this had been Mama's idea. "We don't want you to get all involved in other things. We want you to keep in mind the way things work." He didn't sound like her kind father but like someone chilly and calculating. Sally felt trapped.

They wanted her to marry Nat Wald. Because he was handsome and rich and she'd live in a nice house and they could be proud of her.

But she did not love Nat Wald.

She supposed she could learn to love him. Anyway, love was just in stories. You got along. You had children. You had a home. You and your husband didn't have to have passion . . . passion was not for women anyway. You settled.

The words were not said, but Sally heard them anyway. She'd seen the story acted out among her mother's friends.

Come to think of it, her parents and the Jacobses were the only adults she knew who seemed really in love with one another.

Aunt Frank and Uncle Abraham . . . now, that was love! Uncle Abraham couldn't keep Aunt Frank out of his mind, and he went all the way back to Cincinnati from Denver to get her. And she just followed him into the wilderness . . . that's what Colorado was in 1863. And the way he respected her. Uncle Abraham didn't think Aunt Frank was crazy, the way some people said, for going around and helping and starting charities. He wanted her to think for herself.

"Now, honey," her father was saying, as if she were a frightened three-year-old, "we don't want you to get all upset about this. Just let it happen. The boy likes you and if you're nice, you could have a wonderful life."

Sally felt as if she were being pushed into a corner.

The buggy turned down an unfamiliar street.

"I need to stop at the hospital. You don't mind, do you?"

As the buggy stopped in front of the small dingy building that served as a public hospital, a nurse came running out. "Doctor, thank God you're here. Mrs. Rabinowitz has taken a turn for the worse."

Dr. Gottesman hastened up the steps into the building, with Sally trailing behind. Daniel's mother. Her heart pounded. Something terrible was happening!

The charity ward was a long dim room with small dusty windows, lined with two rows of beds. It was not dirty so much as shabby. Paint peeled from the walls, the enamel on the iron beds was cracked. Rustlings from dark corners told of the presence of rodents. There was the smell of sickness, from many patients, and of disinfectant. Wide-skirted nurses with blue aprons and starched white caps moved among the patients, tending to those who moaned in pain and those who merely stared from feverish eyes.

A curtain had been drawn around Mrs. Rabinowitz's bed, to separate the dying from the living. As Sally followed her father through an opening in the curtain, he gave her a startled disapproving glance; he had expected her to remain outside. But Dr. Gottesman had more urgent concerns than Sally.

The woman in the bed was barely breathing in painful convulsive gasps. Daniel sat by her side, holding her limp hand, grief and hopelessness marking his face. When he saw Sally, he half rose, with a ghost of excitement flickering in his eyes.

"She had a massive hemorrhage this morning," the nurse whispered to Dr. Gottesman. Sally knew her father was trying to look wise and competent as he did his doctor things, taking the woman's pulse and listening to her heartbeat. But everyone, most of all the doctor, realized there was nothing he could do. Disease had eaten away at the woman's lungs until they could no longer function.

In spite of Dora Rabinowitz's parchment complexion and ravaged look, Sally was astounded to see that Daniel's mother was very beautiful, a woman in her thirties with a lovely heart-shaped face and luxuriant dark hair. When she opened tired eyes for a moment, Sally noticed with a pang that they were intense green . . . Daniel's eyes!

Gradually, Sally moved around the bed until she stood next to Daniel. She wanted to comfort him, but didn't know how. It didn't seem right to speak.

In her mind, she willed a cover of safety, an enfold-ment for him. He felt it and sighed, just a little.

Dr. Gottesman turned to prepare an injection that would at least temper his patient's pain. At that moment, Daniel did a curious thing. He took hold of Sally's hand and bent over the bed.

"Mama."

Slowly, his mother opened her eyes. Daniel pulled Sally closer.

"Mama, this is Sarah, the *shayne maydel*."

A tiny smile moved over his mother's lips and she raised one hand, just a little, as if to bless, before it fell helplessly back onto the coverlet.

As Dr. Gottesman turned around, Daniel quickly let go of Sally's hand and she moved discreetly away from him.

Light footsteps were heard coming through the ward. The curtain parted and Frances Jacobs entered. "Your landlady sent word," she said to Daniel, nodding to Sally and Dr. Gottesman. "I'm here to help you."

"Thank you," he said.

Frances looked at Dr. Gottesman. "Sig?"

He shook his head helplessly.

"Doctor!" said the nurse sharply.

Dr. Gottesman quickly placed his hand on Mrs. Rabinowitz's neck. "She's gone."

Gently, he prodded Sally and ushered her through the curtain. Frances Jacobs followed.

"Look at this ward!" the doctor said through

clenched teeth. "They do their best, but this is no place for tuberculosis patients. They must have fresh air, clean bright surroundings, nourishing food. That is the only way we can treat the disease. Someday, we will conquer it, but now we need a place just for them, where they can be treated properly. And a place where children—I see so many children, undernourished children in danger of contracting the disease—can have a chance to be built up."

"The people who come here are destitute," Frances reminded him.

"I know that," he said savagely. "That's why they're sick. So many of them are Jews. They're our people, Frankie. They run from the pogroms and they go to New York and they live in those damn tenements without light or air and they work in the sweatshops making clothes. Tuberculosis is a disease of poverty . . .We need to build a hospital. The Jews of Denver must do this."

"Some of the sick are not Jews," Frances reminded him with a smile.

"Since when is Jewish charity limited to our own? Do you question the religion of the women you help in the tents and in the houses on Market Street?" He put an arm around her and gave her a squeeze. "We're going to do it, Frankie. You and me . . . especially you, with your golden tongue. We're going to wake up the Jews. It's time they stopped ignoring this problem."

Daniel joined them, red-eyed. Slowly, they

walked with him out of the hospital.

"Are you all right?" Frances asked Daniel as they stood on the sidewalk. "Can I drive you somewhere? Are you hungry?"

He heaved a great sigh. "I'm fine. I just want to walk." Then he thought of something. "I need a funeral tomorrow. There is a little *shul* called *Mogen David*."

"I'll take care of it," Frances promised.

"Thank you," Daniel said. He looked around at Dr. Gottesman and Sally. "I thank you to come to help me." He looked straight at Sally, then quickly looked away.

Impulsively, Frances put her arms around him and kissed him. "You are not alone, Daniel."

"Yes." Looking a little embarrassed, he turned and walked slowly down the street.

"I can arrange for the funeral," said Frances. "I think we need to go to it. He'll be all alone."

Dr. Gottesman shook his head. "I can't get away from my office."

"Will you come with me?" Frances asked Sally.

Dr. Gottesman didn't seem very comfortable with that, but it was an act of mercy, a *mitzvah*. He couldn't say no.

The synagogue was very tiny, situated behind a large rag salvage building owned by the son of the rabbi, David Radinsky. Except for the nine strangers recruited from the street to make up the ten men needed for a *minyan*, the gathering included just Frances, Sally, and Daniel.

Along with the rabbi, they rode in Frances' carriage, following the horse-drawn hearse, to the cemetery near Cheesman Park established by pioneer Jews. Slowly, they walked up a hill to where the gravediggers had prepared the grave. The mellow sun of late summer gilded the simple wooden casket as it was lowered into the ground, and the cottonwood leaves sang a requiem. With tears rolling down his cheeks, Daniel threw a handful of dirt onto the casket.

"*Yisgodol*," prompted the rabbi.

His voice getting steadier as he went along, Daniel recited the *Kaddish*, praising God in the midst of sorrow.

After that, they all walked back down the hill to the carriage. The rabbi got a ride with the hearse and Frances drove to the Gottesman house. "Come in and have lunch," Sally suggested.

"I can't." Frances consulted the watch pinned to her shirtwaist. "I have to go to a meeting and I'm late." She gave Daniel a worried look.

"No worry," he told her. "Angel woman. That is what the poor people call you."

Frances laughed. "That's silly." In a more serious tone, she added, "You're sure you'll be all right?"

"All right," he insisted. "Street cars run all over. Soon they will go to Mars." Sally and Frances smiled as he repeated the familiar Denver joke.

As Frances' carriage clattered down the street, Sally and Daniel looked at each other shyly.

"Let's eat," she said at last. Then she had a thought. "Daniel, can you ride a horse?"

"Horses they have in Russia," he answered. "I ride like Cossack."

"I was thinking, we'll take the horses and go on a picnic."

"Picnic. Yes." he sighed.

Sally found some cold chicken and made sandwiches and packed them, along with a few juicy Colorado pears and a somewhat tipsy layer cake made by Ingrid, in a basket. With Daniel on the brown bay, Elmer, and Sally on Stardust, they trotted toward the hidden path, the way to Sally's secret place on the hill.

Chapter **8**

The two horses climbed slowly. The path was narrow and at times wound around boulders. At last they reached the flat place with the old pine tree, and Sally slipped off her horse, brushing her skirt, and Daniel followed. They tied the horses and brought the lunch basket down from Stardust's back, where it had been fastened.

Sally placed a small tablecloth on the rock and spread out the food and urged Daniel to eat.

He sat with his back to the tree, his eyes closed.

"Are you tired?"

"No. I enjoy the air." He took a deep breath. "In New York, the air was bad."

"Your English is much better," said Sally.

"I try." He sat up and took a sandwich. "You tell

me what I do wrong. I must learn. Very fast."

"Why?"

"So you not be ashamed of me."

Sally laughed. "I'm not ashamed of you. I can't speak Yiddish, and just a little German, and you're not ashamed of me."

"I teach you. Listen. You say something important, in Yiddish. '*Hock mir nicht kein chinik.*'"

Slowly, Sally repeated. "*Hock* . . . that's chop. *Mir* . . me. *Nicht* . . . not. *Kein* . . . not also . . . or any. *Chinik*?"

"Teapot."

"Oh." She translated. "Hock me not any teapot. It doesn't make sense."

"I know," he chuckled. "In English, 'Shut up, you're bothering me.'"

It seemed, momentarily, like the sudden shaft of the sun breaking through clouds, that Daniel's heavy anxiety had lifted, and he was his natural young self, full of humor. Sally looked at his mouth, curved in amusement. His lips were full, yet firm, made for laughter.

"*Hock mir nicht kein chinik*," she scolded. "I like it. 'A rolling stone gathers no moss.' That's a silly English proverb."

"A rolling stone gathers no moss," he repeated.

"A person who goes from one thing to another never accomplishes anything."

"Oh. Ac-com-plish-es."

"Means 'does.'"

"Accomplish. I like to accomplish speak very good English."

"I would like to accomplish the speaking of very good English," said Sally. "Or better, I would like to speak English very well."

"You would?" he said solemnly. "I think you speak English very well."

She flipped a pebble at him which he ducked adroitly. They sat with their backs against the tree, eating pears and gazing at the valley. A train chugged along to the south, and a herd of cattle browsed in a vast field below. The mountains had their morning look, very clear, stuck like cloves with pine trees. Far beyond the front range, the granite peaks of the high country were painted orange by the sun.

Sally rested her back against the tree, feeling the warmth of the sun on her arms, her neck, her face, bringing her a feeling of deep peace. She became conscious that Daniel, with his head back and eyes half closed, was feeling the same thing. Another sensation, that had nothing to do with the sun seemed to seep into the pores of her skin and spread to every particle of her body. It was the Daniel essence, as if his life force had become part of her. He turned his head and looked at her steadily and she knew he was feeling the same thing about her.

"Looking at the mountains, it is good," said Daniel, breaking the silence. "Makes me not hurt."

"Healing," Sally remarked.

"Healing. Good word. Like your papa's work. The best work to do."

"Papa can't always heal," said Sally sadly, thinking of Daniel's mother.

"No, a doctor is a man, not God. But," he looked at her intently. "But if the doctor is a good man, like your Papa, kind, it makes the sick person better. In here," and he touched his heart.

"That's important for children, too. I teach in a nursery school; Aunt Frank started it to help little children whose mothers work. At first I couldn't handle the children at all. Then I learned that if you care about each child, one at a time, you can teach a class."

"You have a job?" He was surprised and interested.

"Just for the summer. Maybe I will go to teacher training when I finish high school. I like to teach."

"Tell me what you do, what you teach the children?"

He listened carefully as she spoke, choosing simple words so that he would understand. It was the first time anyone had really cared about her work, except maybe Mrs. Kobey. It was a wonderful, exhilarating feeling.

"You are a good teacher," he said. "You should study and get a job in public school."

A flock of mockingbirds few noisily over their heads and landed in a nearby tree.

"They are beautiful," mused Sally, gazing at the

birds.

"Their black and white design. The way they move. You know, the rabbi told us about a man, a Dutch lens grinder, who taught everything was God."

"Baruch Spinoza," Daniel said. "He was right. But Spinoza thought that if everything was God, we don't need Torah. People are not smart. We need Torah because there are our rules, how to act."

"Do you think God is even inside us, you and me?"

"Yes, the *neshama*, the . . ."

"Soul?"

"The soul. Inside is the soul," said Daniel thoughtfully. "There is a story in Midrash. God decided to give Man part of himself. But it was very very powerful and Man might use the power all wrong. Like a baby playing with matches. People had to learn about it and that would take time. So God decided to hide the *neshama*. But where? He called in all the angels, asking for advice. Should he put it on top of the mountain over there? Or under the ocean? One angel said, 'There is one place Man will never look. Put the *neshama* inside him.' And that is what He did."

Looking at her, Daniel's eyes were brimming with love, as if his very soul shone through. The feeling she'd had before of Daniel's essence swelled and blossomed like a beautiful flower growing from something very pure, the meeting of the *neshama* in each of them. Perhaps this was what was meant when people spoke of what really happened between a man and a woman, who truly cared for one another, not giggling whispers as if it were something shameful.

Automatically, their hands found each other. She could feel the pulse of his blood, meeting her own.

"How do you know so much, Daniel?"

"My Papa, he was a . . . *bucher*." He held his hands in the form of a book.

"A scholar? He studied the Talmud?"

"Scholar. He learned Talmud but many other things too. Read Hebrew, Russian, German, some English. Papa talked to me all the time, telling me things. In Russia it is almost impossible for Jews to go to college. Papa said I must learn, so we came to America."

"It was bad in Russia?"

"Very bad. Someone killed the czar and another czar came, Alexander the third. He told the Cossacks to kill the Jews and they came into the little towns and killed. Papa, he said, 'Let's get out.' So we crossed the border at night. Somebody's baby cried and the soldiers shot at us. The next night we went again and got across. We came in steerage. It was bad. Everybody was seasick. All we ate was herring . . . So we came to the Promised Land." He smiled a half-smile. "It was not Paradise. Papa was a Hebrew teacher. He earned very little. I worked too, carrying things for a dress factory."

"Did you go to school?"

"At night. To learn English. I studied from books from the library, high school things like you learn. But New York was not good. Our home was dark. Smelled bad. Papa said, 'Let's get out of here.' My Papa was a rolling stone but a smart rolling stone. He said 'We go to Colorado'. A man, Saltiel, wanted Jews to start a colony, Cotopaxi. Papa said, 'We will be farmers.' "

"You're lucky you didn't go," Sally remarked. "The Cotopaxi colony failed."

"Not lucky," Daniel sighed. "One day my Papa was crossing the street, his head full of thoughts like always, and he was run over by a wagon, a runaway horse. Then Mama went to work in the sewing place and she got sick. I remembered Colorado, where Papa wanted to go. So we saved money for train tickets and came. But it was too late for Mama."

She asked softly, "Why did you do what you did with your mother? Tell her I was Sarah, the *shayne maydel.*"

"Were you angry?"

"No. You had been talking to her about me, hadn't you?"

"Yes." He seemed embarrassed. "Mama kept worrying. I would be alone. I pretended you were my girl, my *shayne maydel.* She liked hearing about you, about your hair like wheat and your blue eyes. Then God sent you so she could die without worrying."

He became very quiet. His face became flushed, and suddenly he was breathing very hard and he commenced to shake.

For a moment, Sally was paralyzed, in shock. Then, very clearly, she knew what to do. She pulled him toward her and enclosed him in her arms, stroking his back and rocking with him, murmuring "It's all right," not because it was all right but because he needed the rhythm of her words and the sound of her voice.

The shaking subsided and she let go. He moved away from her. "Talk!" she said gently. She had no idea how she knew it, but it seemed terribly important that he put his feelings into words. "Tell me how you feel."

"I—I . . ." He was tongue-tied. Helplessly, he made a motion with his hands like a bird flying.

Sally watched him intently. "You felt as if you were flying apart?"

He nodded

"Emotion," she said. "It's all right."

He blinked and hung his head. "Sorry."

She put her hands on his shoulders. "No. Not sorry. A stone does not feel. A man feels."

"Yes," he breathed. "Thank you."

"Don't thank me. That is why I am here. To comfort you and to love you."

Abruptly, he pushed her hands away and stood up. "No. You do not love me. I do not want that."

Furiously she scrambled to her feet and faced

him.   "Daniel, if there is anything I hate it's a liar. You are not ever to lie to me, do you hear?"

Proudly, he looked straight at her. "I do not lie."

"Good.   Now I want you to look me in the eyes and say 'Sally, I do not want you.   I do not love you.'"

Silently, he gazed at her, his eyes hungry.

"Say it!" She looked straight into his eyes.

He took a breath and said softly, "Sally, I want you. I love you.

"That's better," she laughed and put her arms about his neck. They clung together and it seemed to Sally that their kiss was not only lips meeting, but everything that was herself merging with Daniel, an emptying and a filling and a merging.

 He pushed her away. "This is no good. I do not have time for you. I have no life. Do you understand? I must get my life. You stay with your own friends. Leave me alone."

He pulled away and jumped to his feet. "I must go to work." He walked to the bay horse and untied him and mounted, waiting for her.

Sally just stood there and then picked up the remnants of the picnic and put it in the basket and tied the basket to Stardust's saddle.

When they reached the house and put the horses back in the field, they faced one another.

"Thank you," he said formally, and started to walk down the street toward the horsecar.

"Daniel."

He turned but did not come back to her.

"Are you angry at me?"

"No. Never anger at you." And he kept on walking.

Stumbling, blinded by sudden tears, she went into the house and headed for the kitchen, where Ingrid was cleaning pots and pans. "Sally," she exclaimed. "Why are you crying? Who hurt you?"

"Daniel," Sally sobbed, and blurted out the whole story.

"He said he loved me, so if I told him I loved him too, you'd think that would make him happy."

Thoughtfully, Ingrid tapped her foot, thinking. "I saw this boy," she said at last. "A good boy. But how can he go with you? With all your fancy friends. He feel like a fool. And this boy doesn't want to be a fool. Not this boy."

"I like him better than my friends," Sally said stubbornly.

Ingrid shook her head. "You think so. But you would be very lonesome without your friends. And the Mama and the Papa, they wouldn't like. You would be very unhappy."

"But he said he loved me!"

"Of course. If he loves you, why would he want to make you unhappy? Sally, forget this boy. It will hurt a little, but after a while the hurt will stop."

It was a strange summer. Outwardly, it seemed to be the happiest of times. As she began to understand the children better, Sally enjoyed her time in the nursery school more and more. On weekends, Nat was constantly attentive. In the midst of the crowd of young people Sally had known since early childhood, they enjoyed the many attractions of the summer city. There were long rides into the mountains for picnics and hiking and there was swimming at Cherry Creek Lake. That was sort of fun, but Sally envied the boys, who went churning out into the water, showing off their muscles, cavorting around in the middle of the lake like a pod of dolphins. She had been taught to swim by her brothers, but such things were considered indelicate for young ladies. They needed to stay near the shore, bundled up in frilly bathing costumes and long black stockings, girlishly shrieking and frivolously splashing each other.

In the evenings there were outdoor concerts and dancing and roller skating under the new electric lights.

Sally tried to look forward to each new excitement, and to the casual observer it would seem that no one was more exuberant than she, danced more dances, laughed more uproariously, or was more daring, not afraid to hitch up her skirts and climb the steepest slopes.

But beneath it all she had the uneasy feeling that she wasn't living at all. Except for the time spent teaching, it seemed that everything was make-believe; all of her surroundings were but cardboard scenery like those at the Tabor Grand Opera House. She had lines to say, coy flirtatious words that made Nat feel important. And she had lines she never said because they would upset him.

Lurking beneath her surface gaiety was the memory of the time on the hill with Daniel. It was such a small thing, she kept trying to tell herself, a silly crush. He had made it quite clear that he could not have her in his life and, when she thought about it, she knew he was right. It was quite possible for her to go downtown as she had once before and find him at his newspaper-selling spot. But he did not want that; he would reject her and she couldn't bear that.

But sometimes at night the feeling would overwhelm her, the memory of that complete kiss coming from . . . what did Daniel call it, the *neshama*, the soul. And she would hug her pillow with longing, weeping for him.

Summer ended and her job at the nursery school ended too. The children said good-by with many tears and a big bunch of black-eyed Susans.

Then school began, her senior year in high school, for most of her friends the last year of school, ever.

Sally was sixteen and it seemed as if she'd been a caterpillar and suddenly, in one day, emerged as something else. She wore her hair up in a bun on the top of her head instead of hanging down her back and tied with a ribbon. Her teachers called her Miss Gottesman. She was a young lady.

But sometimes she unpinned her hair, saddled up Stardust, and wildly galloped across the fields and up the hill to the pine tree, where she'd sit and think about Daniel, the look in his strange green eyes, the warmth of his arms about her. It was September, when summer lingers in Colorado with endless sunshine. The mountains had turned golden with aspens, forever turning their leaves to the glinting sun. But he was not there to share it. In secret, where no one could see her, she cried.

She told no one but Ingrid about Daniel, not even Carrie.

Sally laughed a lot and looked for good times. That autumn, there were dances and parties and the theater. Once, riding with Nat in his phaeton through twilight streets on the way to the Tabor Grand Opera House, she saw Daniel, still selling his newspapers.

That night, the play at Tabor's was "Leah, The Jewess," and Sally had been curious to know how a Jewess would be portrayed on the stage. She sat there, in the magnificent theater which Eugene Field had called "modified Egyptian Mooresque" because of its opulence, its marble and fine fabrics and stage curtain gaudily painted with a scene of the ruins of ancient Rome. She was wearing white flowers Nat had given her, and to all the world she looked like a young woman to be envied. The curtain went up on a rather silly play about an old Jewish man who somehow had lots of money and a beautiful young daughter whom he kept a prisoner because he didn't want anyone to take her away from him. Sally heard little. She was reliving the tiny moment when she'd seen Daniel dimly in the twilight as the horses trotted past.

When Nat took her home, he made no move to get out of the carriage. "Wait," he said. "Let's talk."

"All right." It was a beautiful night, commencing to be cool and very clear, the stars etched in multitudes.

"You looked very beautiful tonight," he said.

"Thank you." She was wearing her first really grown-up dress, of mauve taffeta, with a bustle and puffed sleeves.

He pulled her close to him and kissed her, hard, on the lips.

"You never seem to respond when I kiss you," he complained.

"I'm a respectable girl," she said demurely.

He gave her a shrewd look. Then he shrugged. "I'm sorry. I know women have different sensibilities, and you were gently raised."

Sally looked up at him with what she called her wounded fawn expression.

Firmly, he took both of her hands. "Sally, you and I have been going out together for a long time, six months."

"That's not so long," she said swiftly.

He ignored her. "I thought maybe you and I . . . Everyone expects it. We could be engaged."

She pulled her hands away in shock. "I'm only

sixteen!"

"So's Carrie. She's engaged to Simon."

"No, really, Nat." She tried to make her voice sound reasonable. "I've enjoyed teaching so much, I've decided to go to college. Evelyn Jacobs says she can help me get a job when I graduate."

"Are you crazy?" he shouted. The startled horses whinnied. "They don't let married women teach. It's against the school board rules."

"And a silly rule it is," she snapped. "But there you are. I will not be ready to be married for a while."

"Are you playing games with me?" He grabbed her wrist.

"You're hurting me!"

He released her hand. "Good. It'll teach you a lesson. I don't want you to become a spinster school teacher. I want you to be my wife."

"I never said I wanted to be a spinster, although I can't see anything disgraceful about that. I just want a few years to be . . . to be me, before I get married."

He got out of the carriage and came around to open her door and helped her out. "It's that Frances Jacobs who's given you these idiotic ideas," he declared as they walked up to the front door. "Just because her daughter isn't married . . ."

"That's unworthy." Sally stamped her foot in anger. "Aunt Frank is the noblest woman in Denver. She's going to build a hospital for all the poor consumptives."

He laughed. "She is, eh. With her own itty bitty hands?"

"My father is helping her. Lots of other people, like Mr. Mears. They're raising money."

"They'd be better off to raise money to ship those beggars back to where they come from."

Furiously, Sally turned and took her door key from her purse.

Nat took hold of her shoulders and said in a softer voice, "Will I see you next weekend?"

"I promised to help out at the temple fair."

"That's right. See you at the fair. If you sell kisses, I'll buy a dozen."

She couldn't help laughing. He grabbed her and kissed her again. "Just wanted a free sample."

The "Jewish Fair" at Armory Hall, to benefit Temple Emanuel, had received a good deal of newspaper publicity and the citizens of Denver turned out in droves. On each side of the floor, booths displayed donated merchandise to be raffled off. There was food and there was entertainment, including songs by the Shwayder boys, Mary Kobey's talented grandsons. At a Turkish booth, coffee and cigars were sold and a valuable Meerschaum pipe offered for raffle. Gypsy fortune tellers—in another life, Carrie Rosenthal and Lena Wald—told wild and improbable fortunes of sudden wealth and romantic love. There were oil paintings and quilts and hand-woven items and hand-painted china and hand-sewn little girls' dresses, all created by the ladies of the temple.

Dressed in biblical fashion, Sally presided as Rebecca at the well, selling lemonade. The crowds seemed to be pressing in on her. Although it was late October, the hall was very warm and people were thirsty. She took money, poured lemonade, said thank you and poured lemonade. Her pitchers were emptying.

"Ephraim," she called to her brother, "get more lemonade."

The lemonade business was dominated by Gottesmans. Over in a corner, Clara sweated as she squeezed and squeezed and squeezed, while her sons kept bringing more lemons.

"Could I have a lemonade, please?"

Sally turned from calling to her brother toward the customer. "We're just out . . . Daniel!"

"Come," he pulled her hand.

"But I have to stay in my booth."

"You're out of lemonade."

She followed him out of the brightly lit room to a dim corner of the vestibule.

"I had to see you," he said. "I am going away."

"Away?" She clutched at his jacket. "Where?"

"It's very good. The people at B'nai B'rith, they got me a job in a mine. Good money."

"What mine?" she demanded.

"Guggenheim. The Minnie, at Leadville."

"Leadville!" she wailed. "It's so far. And it's high up, Daniel. It will be very cold in the winter. And they have accidents in mines. Oh Daniel, be careful." Tears were running down her cheeks.

He took her by the shoulders. "Foolish *maydel*. Don't you see? Now I am a nothing. I have to make money so I too can be a something. "

"I'll wait for you," she sobbed.

He stroked her hair. "No, you don't wait for me. You live a good life. I just wanted to see you one more time."

He backed her into a corner where they could not be seen and put his arms about her. He kissed her, first her two eyes, then her cheeks, and finally, her mouth.

Then, abruptly, he let her go.

"Good-by, *Shayne maydel*," he said and turned and walked out the door.

ᴡᴡᴡ *Chapter* 9

Suddenly, as is its habit, winter chased away Colorado's mellow autumn. Before Thanksgiving the small snows came, just powdering newly bare trees. Then, as December proceeded, the heavy snows appeared, first in the high country of the Western Slope, then to the little mining communities in central Colorado, and finally to the east, to Denver and the Front Range.

Sleigh bells made the streets of Denver merry and Christmas decorations festooned the stores and homes. In the Jewish community, there were latke parties and dances and Chanukah menorahs. Freight trains coming up from Trinidad in southern Colorado were loaded with coal for the pot-bellied stoves of the poor and the steam heat furnaces of the well-to-do.

But there were those who were too poor to buy coal. The families in the ramshackle homes and tents along the Platte were freezing. Women in the synagogues and churches busily knitted and sewed warm garments for children. Among volunteers from her relief organization, Frances Jacobs, driving a borrowed wagon, shuttled back and forth delivering blankets and coal. Sally and Clara often went with her to help out.

Sally noticed that Aunt Frank was always ready with a smile, a joke, a treat for the children, but there were times when she threw up her hands.

"It's just too much," she declared one evening during dinner at the Gottesmans' home. "There is just too much misery."

Dr. Gottesman sighed. It was a rare event for him to have dinner with his family. All of Denver clamored for a doctor's services for their winter colds and flus.

"Have some more roast beef, Sig," urged Clara. "You need your strength."

"The worst are the consumptives," said the doctor. "It's the old story; they come here to die in our streets."

"Reluctantly, our B'nai B'rith lodge has sent word to lodges across the country, especially in New York, begging them to discourage people from coming to Denver for their health," said Uncle Abraham, nodding his thanks as Sally refilled his cup with hot tea. "We just can't take care of them."

"I suppose it's necessary," Doctor Gottesman sighed, "but it would be good if B'nai B'rith put forth some more effort raising funds for the tuberculosis hospital."

"Sig, you know B'nai B'rith has always favored a tuberculosis hospital," said Uncle Abraham defensively. "They passed a resolution to that effect as early as 1878."

"But we need money. Now!" Dr. Gottesman speared a piece of beef as if it were an enemy and put it on his plate. "There's something wrong with our fund-raising, Frankie. What about newspapers, publicity?"

Frances threw up her hands in mock horror. "And publicize the fact that Denver has a problem it can't solve? Oh, horrors! The City Council would not like that."

"Idiots!" The doctor bit into a slice of meat.

"I don't see why you're focusing only on the Jewish community. Why can't this be an all-Denver project?" asked Clara mildly. "There are wonderful people out there, like Father Ryan, who also care about the unfortunate. "

Dr. Gottesman gazed at his uplifted fork as if it contained wisdom. "I don't know why, Clara, but I just feel it's right for this to be a Jewish hospital. Not to get all sentimental over it, remember that I came here from Germany and I appreciate what America means to the Jews. I want us to pay back in a small way, give a gift to the consumptives, Jew and gentile. We have a beautiful dry climate with lots of sunshine. I know people come from all over the country because of that and it's burdening us. But we were meant to share what we have and this is where we are. I see it as an opportunity for the Jews of Denver to express their love of America."

Embarrassed by this emotional outburst, the doctor bent busily to cutting his meat.

"Why only Denver?" questioned Frances. "Sig, I think we've been limiting ourselves. There are Jewish communities all over Colorado. Don't you think they can contribute to a Jewish hospital, that they'd be proud of that?"

"That's true," acknowledged the doctor. "After all, the people in Leadville, Colorado Springs, and Pueblo belong to us too. The only problem is reaching them. We're all so busy."

"We need a knight in shining armor," said Clara dreamily and then laughed with the others at her fantasy.

"It's going to happen, Sig." said Uncle Abraham. "It will. We just have to try harder. You have my word that B'nai B'rith will do everything in its power to generate funds."

"I guess I'm just an emotional woman," said Frances with a self-mocking expression, "but I always think of things in terms of individuals instead of just looking at the whole picture. I keep remembering that lovely young woman who died."

"Dora Rabinowitz," Sally supplied, a little too

quickly. Her father gave her a penetrating glance.

"Yes, Dora Rabinowitz. Remember, Sally, you and I went to the funeral. She had that nice son, poor kid left all alone. A hospital might have saved Dora Rabinowitz. I think we owe it to her memory to save others like her."

When the Jacobses left, Dr. Gottesman beckoned to Sally. "Could I see you for a moment?

Uneasily, she followed him into his study.

He didn't mince words. "This Rabinowitz. You remembered the woman's name."

"I have a good memory." Sally could feel a blush creeping up her cheeks.

Dr. Gottesman never shouted, but when his voice became icy it was worse than a shout. "Don't keep things from me, Sally. I saw you holding that boy's hand in the hospital. You had been in contact with him after Frances brought him to the house; I could tell you weren't strangers. And then someone told your mother she had noticed you talking to him at the Temple fair."

"Who saw me?"

"If you must know, it was Lillie Kramer."

"She'd say anything to get me in trouble. She's jealous because I go with Nat and she wants him."

"That's just my point," Dr. Gottesman said softly. "Sally dear, your mother and I want only the best for you and we're very pleased with your connection with Nat. I've told you that. Think, you can have a wonderful future as the wife of a rich man. If you start running after this, this, ragamuffin boy, this . . ."

"Daniel," Sally said quietly.

"Daniel . . . you can ruin things with Nat. He won't stand for it. And you just said yourself that there are other girls just itching to attract him. Don't take him for granted, Sally. Stay away from that riffraff." His voice became milder. "I suppose that's not fair. I'm sure he's a good lad. But he's not for you, Sally."

"Don't worry," she said bitterly. "He's not here anymore. He went to the mines."

Her father looked at her warily. "How do you know?"

She backed up, flustered, thinking fast. "He told me, that night at the fair. Uh, he remembered that I had come with you when his mother was dying and he wanted to thank you for your kindness."

"Why didn't you tell me then?"

"I forgot."

Her father studied her shrewdly, detecting the transparent lie. Then he sighed, unwilling to argue anymore. "All right, Sally. I'm glad the young man is gone. If you got tangled with him, it would have been most unfortunate. I only speak of these things because I love you. I want you to have an easy life. You have been sheltered. You don't know what poverty can really be like. Watch out and don't do anything unwise."

"I won't do anything foolish," she promised.

There was nothing foolish about Daniel. But maybe it was absurd for her to worry so much about him and miss him. After he had said good-by that night of the temple fair, she had watched, through tear-dimmed eyes, as he went swaggering out the door, Daniel determined to conquer the world. But then she thought, tears were useless. She needed to figure a way to keep in touch.

It would be bitter cold in Leadville, with an altitude of 10,000 feet. A muffler! A Chanukah present. If he had any manners at all, he'd write and thank her and she'd write back. The next day she bought thick wool yarn in a bright red color, to cheer him up. She worked on the muffler in every spare moment, enjoying its thickness and softness as the muffler took shape. He could wrap it around and around his neck for extra warmth and wind the end around his face to protect himself from bitter wind. The work contented her. It seemed as if she herself would be keeping Daniel warm.

She sent it off from the post office with a brief note: "Happy Chanukah. Love, Sally."

Then she waited to hear from him. At the end of January no letter had come. Maybe the package had been lost . . . but it had her return address on it. Maybe Daniel wasn't at the Minnie mine anymore. Or maybe . . . maybe he just didn't want to have anything to do with her.

But still she didn't give up hope. The mails between Denver and Leadville were uncertain. A letter might come.

She needed to be careful. Her father had expressly told her he wanted her to have nothing to do with Daniel. If he saw a letter from him there would be a scene.

The day after the confrontation in her father's study, Sally found Ingrid dusting the sitting room, or, rather, singing a raucous Swedish song, lightly touching the furniture with a feather duster. Sally pulled her into a corner and whispered, "Do you remember the red muffler I knitted for Daniel and sent to him?"

Ingrid nodded. "It was beautiful."

Sally sighed. "Daniel never wrote to thank me. But maybe a miracle will happen and I'll hear from him. Now, remember this." She leaned close to Ingrid. "You bring in the mail every day. If any mail ever comes from Daniel, from Leadville, please take it aside and keep it for me. It's important that Papa doesn't get hold of it. He doesn't like me to have anything to do with Daniel."

"Yah." Ingrid bobbed her head and put a finger to her lips. She loved a secret, especially a romantic secret.

"And why are you singing so happily?" Sally asked her.

Ingrid pulled a letter from her apron pocket. "Lars, he come. To Colorado!"

Sally threw her arms around her friend. "I'm so glad for you. But, does that mean you'll leave us?"

"Not yet," Ingrid sighed. "I must work and Lars must find work. We save money for our farm."

"But you will see him. That's the important thing."

How lucky Ingrid was, thought Sally as she went to her room. She could see Lars and no one was telling her that he was bad for her. And Carrie, how lucky she was, planning her trousseau and her wedding to Simon.

Everyone was lucky but her.

Why did she have this . . . this sickness, this yearning for Daniel? He didn't even have the courtesy to acknowledge a Chanukah gift. A gift made with her own hands!

She lay down with her face in her pillow and sobbed.

She'd show him. She'd marry Nat. Then he'd be sorry.

But that was exactly what Daniel wanted her to do, to marry Nat. So did her parents.

So she'd marry Nat. Everyone would be happy. And she'd be miserable.

What difference did it make? In despair she kicked her feet against the hand-made patchwork quilt. No one in this world was as unhappy as she was!

But the very next day the letter came. When Sally arrived home from school, Ingrid stuck her head out of the kitchen door and beckoned elaborately. Sally ran into the kitchen and fairly snatched Daniel's letter from Ingrid's hand. Barely thanking her, she rushed to her room to read it.

He had written:

Dear Sally,

Thank you for the muffler. It is most beautiful and it keeps me warm. It is cold here. I work hard and I have many friends. Mr. Guggenheim gives me books and I study every day. My friend Bob helped me write this letter in good English. I hope it is o.k.

Your friend, Daniel Rabinowitz

So . . . he had written. He liked the muffler. He had many friends. He didn't need her. He was her "friend."

She had signed her note "love."

Idly she looked out the window. She was being a fool. The best thing would be to forget this boy. Her father was right.

Out in the yard a ragged looking Indian had come through the gate and was walking toward the back door where Ingrid would give him some of the bread and cheese always put aside for beggars. For it was written in the Torah that the stranger must be fed.

Who is the stranger, she mused, the Indian or the white man? Utes and Arapahoes had once hunted through here. But now the white man had taken the land and most of the Indians had moved on. Stragglers like this man were left to beg.

She thought of Aunt Frank's friend Otto Mears, the famous Pathfinder, builder of roads. He was a friend of the great Ute Chief Ouray, and Mr. Mears had arranged the treaty whereby the Utes agreed to give up their lands and move to Utah. The white men knew there were valuable minerals—gold and silver and coal—under the ground. So they arranged to "give" the Indians land in Utah.

Was that fair?

Feeling more and more melancholy, Sally fingered the tassels on the green curtains at her bedroom window and thought of the miserable families she'd seen by the river, where the children were always cold and hungry.

She was a selfish girl to complain and dwell on her troubles.

Much calmer, she sat down on her flowered rocker and held Daniel's letter in her hands, tracing the letters with her fingers. What was he really saying?

Well, first of all, he was writing the letter with the help of someone else. He'd be embarrassed to be too personal.

She frowned. She wasn't getting to the heart of the matter. She leaned back with her eyes closed, rocking gently. In a rush the feel of Daniel's warm lips kissing every part of her face came back to her. A tear rolled down her cheek and she wiped it away with her sleeve.

He loved her. Of course he did.

Then why was he pushing her away, why did he keep telling her to forget him, to "go with her friends?" By that, she supposed he meant Nat; he'd seen her in Nat's carriage. Rocking, she concentrated on unraveling Daniel's thinking.

She had always looked at the situation from her own point of view. But how did it seem to him? Daniel had a hard road to travel. He had no family to help him, he barely knew English. But he had to make a place for himself.

That was why she loved him, because of his determination to better himself, and his intelligence; she respected him. No, she smiled wryly, it was because of his beautiful green eyes, and his dark hair that felt like silk.

She forced herself to go back to thinking logically, from Daniel's point of view. He didn't need a girl to hold him back.

He did love her. Her Papa loved her too. They both wanted things to be easy for her.

She picked up the rag doll she'd had since babyhood and shook it. "Daniel's a fool," she told her doll fiercely. "Doesn't he know that I'll wait for him until he does what he needs to do?" She thought of the words she had used the day of his mother's funeral. "That's why I am here, to comfort and to love you."

He had pushed her away then and he was pushing her away now. There was no way to make him understand.

February came with its strange springlike days followed by snowstorms and freezing winds, and then March and the snow began to thaw. Strange machines appeared on Denver's streets, spreading

a base over the muddy roads and then pouring on
sticky asphalt. Gradually, the city's streets were
being paved. People were talking about Alexander
Graham Bell's remarkable invention, the telephone. A person could talk to another blocks
away. Dr. Gottesman thought of installing one; it
would certainly be quicker than being summoned
by messenger. But then, Clara pointed out, who
would call him? So few people had telephones.

"It's just not practical," Clara argued. "The
machine is tinny, hard to hear. You have to shout
into the thing. It's just a novelty. It will never succeed."

More and more, electric lighting was being
installed, in street lights and in some homes, replac-
ing gas lighting. The city now had the Power and
Light Company. Engineers were needed to super-
vise the new technology. Simon had graduated
from the School of Mines with an engineering
degree, but instead of going to the mines he had
taken a job with the city in the Department of
Public Works.

Carrie was overjoyed. "We're looking for a
house," she bubbled. "I'd like to get married right
away but my parents insist that I graduate from
high school."

"It's only a few months until June," Sally reminded her.

She had been giving a lot of thought to what she
was going to do after graduation.

"I loved working with the children so much, I

think I'd like to do that," she told Frances Jacobs, one afternoon as they were returning from bringing medicine to a sick woman in West Colfax.

"Splendid!" Frances reached over and hugged Sally. "Miss Griswold has said that you are a natural teacher. But to teach in the public schools, you need special training. The University of Denver has a good course. After two years you'll be eligible for your teaching license."

A March wind blew the bare branches of trees in a crazy dance. Frances held the reins more tightly

Sally tucked the lap robe more firmly around them. "My family wants me to marry Nat," she said pensively.

Aunt Frank's brown eyes studied her carefully. "And does Nat want to marry you?"

"I suppose," Sally shrugged. "He's always talking about getting engaged."

Thoughtfully, Frances gave Blackie, her horse, a light tap with the whip to speed him up a bit. "And so . . . the big question. Do you want to marry Nat?"

"I don't know," said Sally uneasily. "His behavior bothers me. He can be very surly, and he acts as if he owns me. You should have seen him at the Valentine's Day dance. He wouldn't let me dance with anyone else. And then he told me my dress was too immodest and forbade me to wear it again."

Frances shook her head. "Doesn't sound very good to me. If he irritates you now, how could you

stand being married to him? Marriage is a very inti-
mate relationship, Sally. The best marriages are
built on love, where everything is a joy. But marriages based on respect work too. It doesn't sound
as if you and Nat respect each other, much less love
one another."

Glumly, Sally stared through the glass wind
screen of the carriage. Irrelevantly she noticed the
way Frances' horse's ears twitched—Blackie was a
good horse. Why did the thought of Nat make her
feel heavy inside and the thought of Daniel make
her feel like thistledown? But she couldn't have
Daniel . . . .

"I don't know what to do!" she cried, confused.

"Nat Wald is handsome and rich and the woman
who marries him will be important in Denver. It's
tempting. Right?" said Frances.

Sally nodded dully. She hadn't even been thinking of that. If she broke off with Nat, she'd miss out
on all the fun. Who would take her to parties and
dances? There were other boys, but most of her
friends had already paired off.

"Sally darling, you have to think of your whole
life," said Frances, as if she'd been reading Sally's
mind. "You're not even seventeen. At least, tell
him to wait a little while."

"I'll do that," promised Sally. Time, that was
what she needed. "Meanwhile, I'm going to write
to the University of Denver and find out about the
teacher training course."

Several days later Sally's father called her into his study. Her mother was sitting there, looking very pleased. Her father was beaming.

"Sally, great news." He rubbed his hands.

She waited with interest. Perhaps the Messiah had arrived.

"Nathan Wald and his father came to see me. He has asked formally for your hand in marriage."

Sally sat down in a chair, hard. She was filled, not with shock and surprise, but with rage. She was amazed at the extent of it—red, unreasoning fury. "How dare he!" she shrieked. "I never gave him permission to come to you. How can you sit there and try to force me into a marriage I don't want? Do you think this is the Dark Ages, when people sold their daughters?" And, to her disgust, she burst into a torrent of sobs.

"Sally," said Clara soothingly, "Of course we don't want you to marry anyone you don't love. But you have been going with this boy for so long . . . we expected, we supposed, that you cared for him. He's a wonderful boy. Intelligent. And he comes from such a fine family. It would be so nice . . . you married to Nat and Carrie to Simon and, hopefully, Ephraim soon to a fine girl. You would all be friends and your children cousins. Such good times we'd all have!"

Sally gave her mother a long look. "You marry him," she said bitterly and ran from the room into the living room.

Looking through the front window, she saw Nat's carriage pull up in front of the house. He got out slowly, and walked without his usual strut, hesitantly. He was coming to hear her decision and he was afraid.

Her anger at him evaporated and was replaced by pity. He loved her and wanted her. Who was she to mock that when she'd been through so much pain herself?

She opened the door and went out on the porch and greeted him gently.

"I'm sorry, Nat. My parents have told me, but I cannot marry you. We are too different. It wouldn't work."

He stood there, looking at her, blinking.

"Come in," she said. "It's chilly out here." He followed her into the house to the parlor. He grabbed her hands. "Sally, I'll make you love me," he said hoarsely. "I know I've not always been so polite to you and that you don't like to be bossed. I'll try not to do that, I promise!"

She released her hands from his grasp and sat down on the horsehair sofa. "There's nothing wrong with you, Nat. It's just that I feel I'm not ready to settle down. I'm going to teacher training and I do want to teach for a few years before I get married."

"You'll be an old maid" he said savagely.

"I don't think so. Anyhow, what's so bad about that? Susan B. Anthony is a spinster."

"Who?"

"Only the most famous woman in America. She's leading the fight for women's suffrage."

"This is what you want? To go around with crazy women who don't know their place?"

"My mother is involved in the suffrage movement. Do you think she's crazy?"

"We're not talking about your mother. This is about you and me. Are you going to stop this nonsense and marry me? It doesn't need to be right away. I'll wait until you're eighteen. That's a good age."

"I don't want to marry you," she said firmly.

He stood in front of her, looking as though someone had struck him.

"I'm sorry, Nat. I don't want to cause you pain, but if I married you and we were not compatible, the hurt would be much worse."

He looked down at his shoes. Sniffling, he said, "Then you won't go out with me anymore."

"I don't think it would be a good idea."

She followed him to the door and, with mild regret, watched him go. There would be no more parties and dances with Nat, no more riding grandly to the theater in his carriage.

She walked back into the parlor and stood in the middle of the room. Barney, wagging his tail, came nuzzling at her knees and, absently, she petted him.

Then she knew what she had to do. She raced up the stairs to her room and stuffed writing paper, pen, envelope, and a stamp into her pocket. Then she ran to the meadow and saddled up Stardust. Racing with the wind, she galloped across the meadow and climbed slowly to the place on the hill under the pine tree where she and Daniel first knew they loved each other.

Chapter *10*

Sally tethered Stardust and sat with her back to the pine tree, as she had done so many times before. The ground was still damp, and mud soiled her dress, but she didn't care.

Quickly, leaning against a flat rock held on her lap, she wrote a letter:

> Dearest Daniel,
> I want you to know that I am finished with Nat Wald. He wanted to marry me but I see that I can never marry anyone but you. I think of you all the time and I miss you so much. If you have forgotten me, that is all right. If you have found another girl I will understand that too. But if you think of me as I do of you, please answer this letter. I love you.
> Sally

Before she could change her mind, she mounted Stardust and raced downhill and over to the mailbox. She slipped the letter into the slot and closed the top with a resounding bang. Done!

Sally took a deep breath to still the trembling that had suddenly seized her. For better or worse, she had taken hold of her own life. Then, quietly, she led Stardust back to her stall and gave her an extra measure of oats.

It was April. Hard buds appeared on the trees and daffodils swayed against the fences. Colorado weather played its usual "now you see me and now you don't" with spring. Then the air grew warm and fragrant. A time for love.

But there had been no answer to Sally's letter.

She sat with her family at their usual joyful Passover *seder,* feeling as if her heart was as barren as the wilderness through which her ancestors had traveled.

"I was a fool," she stormed to Ingrid as yet another week passed. "Why did I throw myself at him? He probably just laughed at my letter, showed it to his friends and bragged about the silly girl in Denver who gave up a match with a rich man to run after him."

Ingrid's fiancé Lars, a blond ruddy-faced giant, shook his head. "Such a man you don't want to marry. He is a selfish one."

Ingrid put her hand over Lars' huge hairy one. "Now, Lars, you don't know Daniel. He is not like that. Sally, you make up things. Have hope. He will answer."

"It's been so long," Sally sobbed. "I don't have hope. I will not marry anybody. I will go to my grave a spinster!"

Ingrid tilted her head thoughtfully. "I think not."

But Sally continued to mope. Nothing pleased her. She avoided Carrie because she couldn't bear to hear the endless chatter about the upcoming Carrie-Simon wedding. She stopped riding up to her special place on the hill; it was too full of memories of Daniel.

Sometimes she saw Nat in his carriage, Lillie Kramer sitting triumphantly beside him. His broken heart had mended rapidly. She wished her own were so easily healed.

Other boys, realizing she was available, asked her out. But they all seemed so pale and boring. Put off by her lack of interest, they didn't ask her again.

Relations with her parents were strained. Yes, they agreed that she should not marry a man she didn't love. Yes, she could go to teacher training. Why not? She had no other prospects.

And then, one day early in May, she came home and there was Ingrid, beckoning wildly. "A letter has come."

The battered envelope, postmarked Leadville weeks ago, had apparently been lost and rerouted.

Sally carried it out to the shade of the porch swing. She sat in the dim cave formed by the woody vines climbing over the side of the porch, the striped canvas pillows of the swing still faintly musty from winter damp. The fragrance of crabapple blossoms perfumed the soft air. Sending the swing creaking idly back and forth, she held the envelope in shaking hands. Her heart pounding, she managed to slit the envelope open.

The letter was scrawled and there were misspellings. It was obvious that Daniel's friend Bob had not helped this time.

He wrote:

> Shayne,
> Your letter came and made my hart so happy. It is not yet spring but for me the spring is here. You will not be sorry. I study very hard. Mr. Guggenheim will help me to go to Colorado Agricultural College in Fort Collins where his brother gave the school a building. After that maybe I will go to medical school. I thought about my life and what I am supposed to do, and it is to be a doctor. I tried to make you forget me because it will take a very long time but if you will wait I will love you my whole life. With many kisses and hugs and loves,
> Daniel

She laughed a little, through her tears. So her name had been changed! For the rest of her life she would not be Sally, but Shayne, at least to Daniel.

Sally longed to tell the whole world about Daniel, but the memory of the discussion with her father, when he had expressly forbidden her to have anything to do with Daniel, stopped her. She must hold her wonderful secret enclosed, safe from ugly controversy. So only Ingrid and Lars, and—after a little while, Carrie—knew what made Sally so joyful.

There were many letters now, all discreetly delivered by Ingrid. Daniel's English vocabulary increased with amazing speed until he was able to tell her about the details of his life, the mines, his friends, the lively town of Leadville.

Sally described her graduation from high school —the procession, the solemn words, the speeches. The valedictorian—the same Milton Silverman who had tormented Rabbi de Sola—pronounced in booming tones that the Class of 1887 would conquer the world, would be the pride of Denver, in fact, of all America. All with appropriate thanks to parents, teachers, and the Board of Education.

She had been accepted into Denver University's teacher training course, she wrote to Daniel, and would start in the fall. Meanwhile, she'd get some extra practice by teaching during the summer in the nursery school. Daniel replied that she was wonderful and that he was proud of her. He wrote that the authorities at Colorado Agricultural College had told him that, while usually they did not accept anyone who had not graduated from high school, they would consider him if he could pass an examination.

"There are many, many things I must learn," he wrote. "Every day Mr. Guggenheim brings me more books. I am studying English and history and mathematics and science. Pretty hard because I don't have much time and some of the words are new to me. My friends help me."

Sally felt a pang of envy of Daniel's friends. If he were only here, she could help him!

Shortly after graduation, the much-awaited Carrie-Simon wedding took place. Sally, wearing pink organdy, was maid of honor. The ceremony was held in the temple, with Rabbi de Sola, uncharacteristically sentimental, delivering a speech about how happy he was to officiate at the wedding of one of his students.

"He's resigning as rabbi," Clara murmured to Sally as they stood, perspiring, under the canopy with the bridal couple. "That's why he's so nostalgic."

The reception was held at the Standard Club, the popular center for Jewish occasions. Afterward there was a long session as a photographer fussed with photographs, ducking under his black canopy, coming out and issuing instructions, ducking back again, and repeating the process, until finally he squeezed the bulb that took the picture. When the photos were developed there was a good one of Sally, which she sent off to Daniel.

The busy summer passed and then there was the excitement of the new school and new friends. They were serious girls, many of them from poor farm families, who wanted to better themselves. They would teach for a few years, they hoped, then find a husband.

Gradually, Sally drifted away from her old friends. Her lifeline was the chain of letters to and from Daniel. There was loneliness and what would seem like an endless wait until he at least got to Fort Collins, which was nearer to Denver. But Sally had a good feeling that she had taken hold of her life. There was purpose and hope.

She enjoyed school and the simple pleasures she shared with her classmates. She dressed like them, soberly, in modest long skirts and shirtwaists, her hair drawn up in a prim bun on top of her head.

But sometimes she looked at her beloved mountains, almost hating them because the rows and rows of peaks separated her from Daniel. She wanted to sweep away the rocks and the gorges and run to him. Once, she even went down to Union Station and inquired about trains to Leadville. She looked out at the tracks leading tantalizingly toward the high country. It was possible, and not possible. Whatever would Daniel do with her if she suddenly appeared? He had enough on his hands. And she could imagine the row it would cause with her father. A single woman traveling alone to a distant city to be with a man she had been forbidden to contact? Sally shuddered at the imagined consequences and regretfully returned home.

The trees had lost their leaves and skies were pewter gray. The long winter and many months lay ahead until she could see Daniel. It seemed to Sally that she couldn't bear it, but she had no choice.

One afternoon just before Chanukah and Christmas, when celebration was in the air, Clara, sitting in the big armchair in the parlor, called to Sally as she came in from school.

"Sally, you're getting old-maidish," her mother fretted. "Why don't we have some pretty dresses made for you?"

"But I haven't been going anywhere to need dress-up clothes."

"I know." Clara put down her needlework, frowning. "What happened to the parties and the dances? Never mind about Nat Wald. To tell you the truth, he rubbed me the wrong way with some of his views. If you fixed yourself up, you could attract someone else."

Sally perched on an ottoman near her mother's feet. "I don't want anyone else," she said dreamily.

Clara looked at her sharply. "It's that boy, Daniel, isn't it? Are you still mooning over him?"

Sally laughed. "I wouldn't call it mooning exactly." She hugged her knees. "I just love him very much and he loves me. I'm going to marry him, Mama."

Clara leaned over and tilted Sally's chin. "I know.

Don't think I haven't noticed the letters that Ingrid thinks she's hiding. Tell me about Daniel, Sally."

"He's got the most beautiful green eyes, Mama."

"A girl doesn't marry a man because he has green eyes," said Clara. "Although," she sighed, "some do. And often regret it. You can't build a life on the color of someone's eyes, or, " she colored a little, "the sweetness of his kisses."

Sally paused, full of longing, thinking of the sweetness of Daniel's kisses. Then she said, "Daniel is dear and sweet and loving, Mama, but he's much more. He's extremely intelligent. His father was a scholar, a teacher. He knows all about Judaism and the sacred books, but he knows other things too. He works in the mines, but he's also studying high school subjects so he can pass an examination and get into college. He wants to be a doctor, Mama, and work in the new hospital."

Clara listened to all this with increasing interest. Then she looked intently into Sally's eyes. "Honey, I didn't think you would ever choose someone without worth. But his plan will take years, if he succeeds. Are you willing to take that chance?"

"Mama, I know it's hard. And Daniel knows it too. He tried to discourage me, but it's impossible. I can't imagine living with anyone but him."

Delicately, Clara inserted her needle to make a French knot. When she looked up, there were tears in her eyes. "You're a grown woman, Sally, and a strong woman. I don't know whether you can understand, but a mother feels strange when she knows that about her child. I guess part of me wants to keep you in pinafores and hair ribbons forever."

"What about Papa?" Sally wondered.

Clara sighed. "Papa trusts you. You've never lied to him until now. But getting letters from a lover is deceiving him. He told you he didn't want you to have anything to do with the boy."

"But I had to disobey him, Mama. I couldn't ruin my life and Daniel's just because Papa has some unfounded prejudice against him."

"Of course not," Clara agreed gently. She ended her stitch and cut the thread with her little gold embroidery scissors. "We'll just not tell Papa anything about it for a while. When the time is right, he'll know. And he'll come around. He must." She grinned. "You are his only daughter."

Impulsively, Sally jumped up and hugged Clara. "I love you, Mama."

Later, as she went upstairs to do some studying, Sally noticed the sun coming through the stained glass window, turning it to glowing jewels. Her heart felt so much lighter, now that Mama knew everything.

Then she stopped on the landing with a catch in her throat. Daniel had no one to confide in, only herself. Here was another element of love—listening and caring.

She sat down at her desk and wrote to Daniel:

Sweetheart,

I know you think of yourself as a strong, brave fellow, but sometimes we all need someone to confide in. Do you remember what I once said to you, that I am here to love you and comfort you? So you don't always have to write to me about funny or interesting things. If you get tired or discouraged or lonely, you can write to me about that too.

And he did. He replied,

Shayne,

Sometimes my lonesomeness for you is so great, it hurts. I would come to Denver to see you but I must save all my money so I can go to school. I cannot leave my work. Sometimes it seems forever. I look at the mountains and hate them because they separate me from you.

Sally smiled as she read the last line. So they had both had the same thoughts! It was not necessary to go on a train journey. You could send your thoughts across the miles instantly!

Immediately, she sat down and wrote to him about that. They arranged that at sunset, every day, they would send thought messages to one another.

Sally became more involved in helping Frances Jacobs in her charitable work and especially in the activities promoting the new hospital. A committee, which called itself the Jewish Consumptive Relief Society, was busy running fund-raising events, sending speakers around, and trying to get publicity into the newspapers.

However, it seemed as though the newspapers had a conspiracy of silence against the hospital. Frances Jacobs visited the editors, declaring, "We need a hospital big enough to take care of these people who walk the streets . . . ill unto death, coughing away what little life is left. It is a reproach to the city and to all of us that when they fall on the street the police patrol comes and the sick man is taken to jail. That is the terrible thing I have seen on Sixteenth Street."

As Frances' ringing tones implored the editors, the City Room fell silent, everyone listening to her, mesmerized. But even Frances Jacobs' golden tongue could not move the editors. Such an article, they felt, would tarnish the image of the city that proudly called itself the "Queen City of the Plains." Although they were often tempted to appeal to the general community, many of whom were also concerned, the Jewish Consumptive Relief Society kept to its stubborn intent: this was to be a Jewish-sponsored hospital, realizing the principle of *tzedakah*—the Jewish obligation to help the unfortunate—in brick and stone. But in spite of the group's efforts, it seemed as if it would take years to finally build a hospital.

The endless months passed and at last Sally and Daniel began to see an end to their waiting. She had finished teacher training and he was about to take the entrance exam that would permit him to go to college in Fort Collins, only sixty miles north of Denver, a mere two-hour train ride.

Something else happened in 1889. Clara's "knight in shining armor" arrived in Denver. He didn't look like a knight. He was only twenty-one years old, newly graduated from the Union Theological Seminary in Cincinnati. His name was William Friedman and he was Temple Emanuel's new rabbi, their first rabbi to have been born in the United States.

He was handsome, with a strong chin, a shining black pompadour, magnetic dark eyes, and a wide sensitive mouth. The hearts of mothers with eligible daughters warmed and the daughters sighed. But Rabbi Friedman's most wonderful quality was his compelling, resonant voice.

He spoke not only of religion but of many things that affected the Denver community. He was interested in the non-Jewish people as well as in his own congregation and quickly made friends with ministers and priests, particularly Father William O'Ryan.

Rabbi Friedman was powerfully interested in helping the distressed and worked with Frances Jacobs to expand her projects. Her tiny kindergarten became a school for a hundred children taught by volunteers, like Sally, from the congregation.

His greatest interest was the proposed new hospital. With his drive and spellbinding voice, combined with Frances Jacobs' speaking ability, they inspired contributors at rallies in Denver and all over the state. Along with other committee members of the Jewish Consumptive Relief Society, they traveled to wherever there were Colorado Jews— Colorado Springs, Pueblo, Grand Junction, Georgetown, Boulder, Greeley—and even to tiny mining camps like Telluride, speaking about the hospital, the gift the Jews of Colorado were to give to their state.

"I think it'll be safe to travel," Rabbi Friedman was saying at a committee meeting one evening in the Gottesmans' dining room.

Sally, taking notes for the meeting and concentrating on beautiful penmanship so that her minutes could be easily read, half heard the rabbi.

"That's true," said Dr. Gottesman. "Leadville. We've been neglecting Leadville."

Hastily, Sally blotted a spurt of ink on the page.

"Who wants to go?" asked the rabbi. "It's a day's journey by train. We'll need to spend a few days."

"I can't get away," said the doctor. "There's an epidemic of chickenpox in town."

Frances said, "I'll go."

There was silence around the table. No one could get away; the beginning of the summer season was busy time for merchants. Abraham Jacobs had given up his O.K. store and had a new job with an insurance company. He could hardly ask for time off.

"I guess it's just you and me, Frances," said the rabbi.

Primly, Sally folded her hands. "I don't think it is proper for Aunt Frank to travel with a young unmarried man without a chaperone."

Everyone stared at her—especially her father, who looked flabbergasted. He had never expected Sally to come to the rescue of propriety and womanly virtue. Good Lord, he thought, Frankie was twice as old as Friedman. But still attractive, he had to admit.

Suddenly emphatic, Clara declared, "It would be a scandal for us to send a man and woman unaccompanied to Leadville." She drew herself up righteously and secretly winked at Sally, who was becoming all flustered with excitement.

Solemnly, with just a hint of a quirk of a smile at the corners of her mouth, Frances agreed. "Yes, Clara, you are perfectly right. I think it would look much better if another woman accompanied us. Sally, would you be free to get away for a few days?"

Sally frowned, as if she were mentally consulting a crowded calendar. "I think so. School is finished for the year and I haven't started my summer work at the kindergarten."

"It's settled then," the rabbi said innocently. "Frances, Sally, and I will go to Leadville."

On the way out of the house, Frances put an arm around Sally's shoulders and murmured. "You'd better write to Daniel and tell him you're coming."

When the committee members left, Sally ran to the stable and saddled up Stardust. She raced into the fields and up to the hill and flung her arms wide. As an eagle came soaring down from a high peak, she cried, "I'm coming, Daniel. I'm coming to see you!"

~~~ Chapter 11

Burdened with luggage and food for the trip, Sally, Rabbi Friedman, and Frances boarded the Union Pacific Leadville Express at 8:40 a.m. For twelve hours the rattly wooden cars steamed over narrow-gauge tracks, especially made to fit the narrow spaces between the mountains. Cinders flew by the windows, and it seemed best to keep them closed although the car was stuffy.

Although she had brought a book to read, Sally kept her face pressed to the window, staring at the panorama of the Rockies. There were fields dense with roaming cattle, and hillsides tinted with spring flowers. With the locomotive tooting to frighten any stray cattle on the tracks, they passed the busy mines near Idaho Springs dotting the hillsides with wooden shanties and buckets to bring the ore up from the pits. Then they went around the famous Georgetown loop, gazing at the majestic peaks of the high country, Engelman Peak, Bard Peak, and Gray Wolf Mountain. Clinging to the side of the mountain, the train chugged over Loveland Pass at almost 12,000 feet and passed fields of snow that never melt. Here and there, a tiny cabin nestled against the side of a hill. A small band of hunting Arapahoe Indians who had camped in a mountain meadow waved at the train. Every so often, an elk would emerge from the pine forests and stand very still, regarding the train with mild alarm.

"There's a fourteen-thousand-footer," Frances pointed out, as the train dipped down to the Arapahoe Basin. "Gray's Peak." A cloud lightly touched the giant peak with its shadow. "The Earth is the Lord's," murmured Rabbi Friedman.

The train stopped at the mining camps at Dillon and Frisco, and the cars filled with noisy, booted miners headed for Leadville and a wild time. Then it turned south along the Ten Mile Range, to Climax camp, and for a distance the tracks hugged the banks of the Arkansas until the train turned from the river, climbing upward to the "Cloud City," Leadville, elevation 10,152 feet.

"What happened here?" Rabbi Friedman exclaimed in dismay as, in fading light, the train wound through bare hillsides. A swirl of foul-smelling sulfurous fumes seemed to engulf the entire valley.

"They've cut down the pine trees to make charcoal for the smelters. The fumes are from the smelters. You notice them more here than in Denver because they're so concentrated," said Frances.

They were met at the station by a gregarious man with a wagon, who introduced himself as Meyer Goldstone, pawnbroker. "Big business here," he commented as he managed to maneuver his wagon through the jammed street. "Pawning. That's how the small miners get their grubstakes. Sometimes they're not lucky and we're stuck with the pledge. Any time you want a watch . . .

"This here street is called Harrison Avenue. It's the main street and I guess the only street worth mentioning."

Branching off from Harrison Avenue, the side streets, lined with little wooden houses, all ran downhill.

They passed numerous saloons, now lit up with gaslight as evening approached. The sounds of brass horns and tinkling pianos and banjos mingled in the summer air. "There's the Lake County Courthouse, built all of brick." Mr. Goldstone pointed out with his whip, "That clothing store over there is owned by Wolfe Londoner of Denver. Know him?"

"He's running for mayor," Frances told him.

"Do tell."

"Say, you've got a Tabor Opera House too!" Sally exclaimed.

"Whaddaya mean too. This here one was built first, after Tabor made his killing in the Little Pittsburgh mine.

"We got a nice little shul here, Rabbi, nothin' like your palace in Denver, but we're all friends. None of this I'm German, you're a Russian, I pray in Hebrew, you pray in English stuff. All together in one happy family." He stopped and reconsidered what he had just said. "No offense, I hope. Denver is a mighty fine city. Spent some time there myself.

"Well, here we are." The wagon pulled up in front of a yellow brick building with a barber pole in front. "Clarendon Hotel. Now you just wash up and I'll come and get you in an hour for the meeting. I just want you to know that the Jews in Leadville are behind your hospital one hundred percent."

Frances and Sally looked wearily and longingly at the neatly made beds in their room, but the audience was waiting. They freshened up and were downstairs and waiting when Meyer Goldstone returned, this time with a handsome two-horse buggy. As they neared Temple Israel, where the meeting was to be held, a splendid carriage came clattering down the street.

"Benjamin Guggenheim, one of old Meyer Guggenheim's sons," said Mr. Goldstone. "Always makes a big splash. That kid who's been driving him is a regular cowboy."

"Looks familiar," said Frances drily, but Sally had already jumped from the barely stopped carriage.

"What's with her?" Mr. Goldstone asked in amazement. "Women throw themselves at Benjamin Guggenheim, why not? Personality plus a bachelor, a millionaire. But this is ridiculous."

"Sally likes cowboys," Frances shrugged.

Unceremoniously, Daniel handed the reins to his employer and jumped from the carriage. Under the stares of an interested crowd he grabbed Sally in mid-flight and hugged her until, flustered by the audience, she pulled away.

"This is my sweetheart, Sally Gottesman," Daniel said grandly to Mr. Guggenheim, who had tethered the horses and, elegant with his silk cravat and pompadoured hair, stood watching them.

"Honored, I'm sure, Miss Gottesman." To her astonishment, he took her hand and kissed the back of it. The onlookers sighed. How continental! "Daniel has mentioned you. In fact," he grinned, "he talks of nothing else. The messiah could appear on Harrison Avenue and Daniel would say, 'Ho hum, have I told you about Sally?'"

Reddening, Daniel swiftly turned to Frances. "This is my good friend, Mrs. Frances Jacobs, who is very famous in Denver for helping others."

"Not at all," fussed Frances. "I'm glad to meet you, Mr. Guggenheim. We know your brother Simon well; he is very active in our temple. And this is our new rabbi, William Friedman."

Frances and Rabbi Friedman were tired from the day's journey, but they became reinvigorated by the reception they received from Leadville's Jews. Frances' emotional plea for compassion for the swarms of poor and ill people who had come to Colorado and the Rabbi Friedman's exalted appeal to the spiritual needs of *tzedakah* brought storms of applause and pledges of contributions.

Sally and Daniel found seats in the back of the temple and held hands, only half-listening to the speeches. "You look so different," she whispered. "You are bigger."

He laughed. "Working hard makes you bigger. And you, you are not changed. You were already the most beautiful girl in the world, so how could you become more beautiful?"

"You're an idiot," she murmured, nestling against him.

"Shhh," said someone in front of them. They moved out of earshot.

"I have been given two days off to be with you," he whispered. "Tomorrow I will bring you to see my friends. And we will go to the opera house to see 'Uncle Tom's Cabin.'"

"You talk differently," she decided. "A sort of Yiddish twang."

"Shh," said another person in front of them.

So they settled down, arms twined, and just gazed at the stars . . . artificial twinkling stars . . . that adorned the temple ceiling.

"Here is where we go down into the mine," Daniel shouted to the visitors the next day at the

Minnie mine, above the creak of the chains bringing miners down in open carriers from a platform into the blackness of the excavation and then hauling up buckets of crude rock containing molybdenum. Wagons trundled the ore to carts drawn by donkeys along a railroad siding. The morning sky was dimmed by the sulfurous fumes from the smelter on the hill. The women sniffed in distaste but Rabbi Friedman was fascinated. He peered into the excavation. "How do you see what you're doing?"

"Candles," said Daniel.

"And fresh air?"

"Special blower tubes. But believe me, it stinks down there. Wet, too. That's why the miners are wearing rubber boots."

"How do you extract the ore?"

"Power drills run with compressed air. Then, dynamite."

Daniel grinned at the alarmed looks of the women.

"Isn't it dangerous?" Sally reached out a hand and touched him as if he were going to blow up at any minute.

"Sort of," he said, strutting a little. "But miners are a tough lot. What will be will be."

Sally wasn't sure that was the answer she wanted to hear. She clutched his hand as they walked down the hill to the waiting carriage. "Can't you get some other job?"

"Well, to tell the truth, I don't go down as often as the other men. Mr. Guggenheim always wants me to drive him somewhere. He's very good to me." He turned to Frances and Rabbi Friedman. "Mr. Guggenheim is making it possible for me to go to the agricultural college in Fort Collins."

"Are you planning to be a farmer?" asked Rabbi Friedman as they took their seats in the carriage, on loan from Benjamin Guggenheim. Daniel gave the whip a sharp crack and the horses galloped dangerously down the steep incline. In the back seat, the women clutched the sides of the carriage with one hand and grabbed their hats with the other.

"No," Daniel answered. "You know that hospital you're building? That's for me."

"Don't feel that way," said Frances. "Medical research has proved that tuberculosis isn't hereditary."

"I don't mean as a patient. After I finish with Colorado Agricultural College, I'm going to medical school."

"That's a hard hill to climb," said the rabbi. Already a Coloradoan, he thought in terms of mountains.

"I've been lucky. People help me."

The rabbi sighed. "I know what you mean. I lost my parents before I was thirteen and was raised in an orphanage."

"Is that so?"

The two young men, almost the same age, looked at each other, understanding one another's determination.

There was no escaping the hospitality of the Leadville Jews. A successful merchant named David May invited them for lunch at his luxurious home. Frances and Sally admired the elegance, surprising in a mining city perched high on a mountain.

"Lots of money in this town," said Mr. May. "I've done well. I'm thinking of opening branch stores of my company—the May Company—in other cities."

"You have culture here too, I see," remarked Rabbi Friedman. "Sally's young man has invited us all to the opera house."

"Culture, yes, in a manner of speaking," Mr. May chuckled. "It'll be an experience." Then he added, "Tabor struck it rich, but he shares his wealth. Donated the land for our temple."

The opera house, opulent in the Tabor tradition, was jammed with miners and some of the sober folk of the town. The theatrical company was performing "Uncle Tom's Cabin," now on its eighth rerun. The people of Leadville never tired of the production, especially the part where live bloodhounds, chasing poor Eliza, were led onto the stage.

The audience clearly was not used to culture with a capital C. They yelled threats at Simon Legree and they laughed when little Eva made her most poignant speeches. At the gripping climax, when Eva was taken up to heaven via wires suspended onto the stage, the audience exploded into applause, catcalls, Colorado whoops, and cries of "Bye bye, Eva!"

"As Mr. May said, it was an experience," laughed Frances as they left the theater.

"The miners don't behave well but they are good fellows," said Daniel. "Come. We'll go to my home and have a drink and meet my friends. They want to know where I'm hiding Shayne. When I show them her picture they say this is not so, that an ugly fellow like me cannot have such a beautiful sweet-heart. They say I stole the picture from an actress."

He drove down a side street to a ramshackle cabin not far from the mine. Over the front door was a sign, "Junk Lane Hotel."

The occupants obviously were expecting them. Bits of clothing revealed where they had been hasti-ly shoved under cot beds. Beside one of the cots, Sally noticed a small table piled high with books, her photo in a neat frame next to them. The floor had been swept, sort of. There were even wild-flowers in a jar in the middle of a home-made table that occupied the center of the one room. A wood stove had been polished with fresh blacking.

Nervously, Daniel found various chairs for the guests, including a plush armchair with springs coming through the seat.

He introduced the other miners, three tall lanky fellows named Bob, Bill, and Vern. Shuffling, the men shook hands.

"This your girl, Dan!" exclaimed Bob. "Told you the picture was a lie. That gal in the picture isn't nearly as pretty as the real one."

The men brought out beer and wine and a platter of hard cookies.

"This is the Junk Lane Band," said Daniel proudly. "They play banjos and guitars and Bob here wrote a song. Want to hear it?"

Bashfully, Bob started to strum on his guitar. "I just wrote the words. Guess you might know the tune—'Home on the Range.' That was in Texas. This is called 'Colorado Home.'"

The other miners joined in loudly with Bob's version of the song.

> "Oh, give me the hill and ring of the drill,
> In the rich silver ore in the ground;
> And give me the gulch where the miners
> can sluice,
> And the bright yellow gold can be found."

The visitors quickly learned the words and soon the little cabin vibrated with raucous voices. The Junk Hill Band played more songs, with everyone swaying in time. Finally Frances declared "If we don't go back to the hotel soon, I shall fall asleep right here on the floor."

As the group headed out to the crisp night, blooming with stars that seemed near enough to touch, Daniel whispered to Sally, "I have the whole day off tomorrow to spend with you."

Early the next morning, Daniel appeared at the hotel. "Mr. Guggenheim loaned me the carriage again. I thought you might like to see some scenery, away from the smelters."

"Sorry," said the Rabbi Friedman. "I have a meeting scheduled."

"I'm exhausted," said Frances. "I think I'll just stay here and read."

"Looks like it's just you and me, Sally," said Daniel. When they got out of sight of the others, he slipped his arm around her waist and helped her into the carriage.

"I didn't think they'd come," he said contentedly. He gave the whip a snap. "Come on, boys, let's go!"

The horses trotted briskly away from the muddy clangorous town and skies surly with the smoke from the smelters. The air was Colorado crystal, the sky a cloudless blue and the sun embellishing everything with marvelous clarity.

Daniel reined in the horses at a grassy patch facing the mountains and brought out sandwiches of thickly cut bread and cheese, a bottle of water, and two tin cups. They settled against a pine tree, reminding Sally of her own special place at home.

Daniel pointed to a huge mountain across the valley, topped by a granite peak. "Mount Ebert, the king of them all, 14,433 feet high. As our ancestor David would say, 'Look to the hills.'"

She sat upright and looked at him, at his deep green eyes, full of a thousand thoughts, brimming with love. "I love you, Daniel," she said.

He pulled her close again, and they did not speak, but just explored the miracle of one another, stroking and kissing and holding. A wind came up through the hills, rattling leaves, like the sound of a faraway train. A file of birds flew overhead, in perfect order.

"Will you marry me, Shayne Maydel?" he asked softly.

"I'll think about it." She lay her head on his chest. He undid the pins in her hair and stroked the blonde cascade. She pulled down his head and kissed him. "I will marry you."

"It'll be a while. In September I go to Fort Collins to the Aggie school. That'll take a few years. Then medical school, if I'm lucky enough to get accepted."

"I'll be an old lady before we can get married," Sally said woefully, biting into a sandwich.

"I'm sorry, Shayne." He sat up and held a sandwich idly between his knees and gazed at the huge mountain. "But that is what I must do, even though it is hard."

She stroked his slightly stubbly cheek. "You must think I'm a spoiled brat. You're doing all the work and I'm complaining."

"It'll be easier now. Fort Collins is only about two hours away from Denver; I checked. I can come to see you."

She sat up and looked across the valley to the huge peaks. "They say that when Moses went up to the mountain he spoke directly to God. Do you think he did, Daniel?"

Daniel lay back with his hands behind his head. "I think so, Shayne. Maybe not the way the old people used to think . . . having a conversation with an old man with a beard. Moses came to know things. He learned what it is our people must do for the world. That is why Frances and Rabbi Friedman and the others want to build a hospital. For a Jew to build a hospital, to help the distressed, to teach as you do, to look for justice, are natural things."

A soft flutter of leaves made them look up. A speckled deer had stepped noiselessly through a stand of aspen and stood looking at them, not afraid, just mildly curious. Then it turned and ducked back into the trees.

"God's messenger," said Sally with a little laugh. She picked up a twig and thoughtfully chewed on it and then threw it away. "Sometimes I'm full of questions and I get on Stardust and I ride very fast and then I go up to my special place, you remember, where I took you, and there I sit quietly and think. Maybe this is talking to God."

Daniel sat up and ceremoniously parted her hair and kissed her on the back of her neck.

Then he clasped his knees and gazed at her. "Yes, " he said. "I too talk to God. I get all upset and I say, 'God, why did you let this happen?' and then God lets me see. Mama was sick and I remembered that Papa wanted to come to Colorado, so I took all our money and I bought tickets on the train. Then when we got here I knew I was a fool. I had no money, we had to live in a terrible place. And Mama was sicker than ever."

Impatiently, he wiped tears from his cheeks. "I'm sorry. I'm a man and I'm not supposed to cry. But I do cry sometimes."

She pulled him close. "Sweetheart, why shouldn't you cry if you hurt? How can you help others if you don't understand their suffering?"

He smiled a little lop-sided grin. "That's true," he sighed. "On the worst day of my life, when I had to bury my mother, when I was so scared, all alone, God sent me a little girl, just a little fifteen-year-old girl and she said 'That's why I'm here, to love you and comfort you.' I hung on to those words like a drowning man."

"But you told me not to love you," she reminded him. "You ran away from me."

He looked at her steadily. "I was so . . . so mixed up . . . I didn't want to involve you, a schoolgirl to be in the middle of my troubles."

"I didn't believe you, did I?" she chuckled.

"Of course you didn't. You knew what was real." He pulled her close and smoothed her hair. "And now, Shayne, now that I know what my life is all about, I must say it back to you. I am here to comfort you and to love you always."

She leaned back contentedly against his chest.

He reached over for the water bottle and poured them each a drink in the tin cups. For a few moments they drank silently.

Daniel remarked thoughtfully, "When I heard about the hospital, I knew that is why God put me on earth, to care for the people in the hospital. I don't mean just give them medicine. Really care for them and help them when they're afraid and when they have pain. That is why you must wait for me, Shayne."

"I know," she said.

"That day, when Mama collapsed and Frances came and brought me to your house, I did not want to live. All of you were so dressed up and you were staring at me, a dirty boy from the street. But then I saw you and you looked right at me and I knew why I was there. I had loved you since I was born and I had to come all the way from Russia to find you."

"But when you were born, I was not born yet," Sally reminded him.

"I loved you before you were born. The Kabbala tells us that our souls do not die, they are forever."

"I knew that too, when I saw you. I had to go down to Joslin's in the city and find you." She turned around and, leaning on an elbow, gazed at him. "If I hadn't come to where you were selling newspapers, what would you have done?"

He laughed. "I would have found you. Nothing would have stopped me." He gently pulled her to a standing position. "Come," he said. "We must go shopping now."

Startled, she followed him into the carriage.

"What do you need to buy."

Daniel addressed the horses. "Giddyap, boys. We are in a hurry. I must buy my Shayne a present."

"Daniel, you mustn't! You must save your money."

He looked at her severely. "Oh, yes I must."

Hitching the horses in front of Cohn's Jewelry Store, he led her into the dim shop.

"Good day, Mr. Cohn," said Daniel importantly.

Mr. Cohn, a small man with wire spectacles, looked at them curiously. "You were at the meeting about the hospital, young lady. You do not live in Leadville, hey?"

"No sir, I came from Denver with Mrs. Jacobs and Rabbi Friedman."

"Such speakers," Mr. Cohn beamed. "Golden voices. A treat for all of us. Myself, I contributed. Generously. The hospital is needed."

"Thank you," said Sally.

"We have come to buy a ring," said Daniel loudly, impatient at the chitchat. "My girl and I are engaged to be married. We need a ring."

"Is that so!" exclaimed Mr. Cohn, as if he'd never met an engaged couple before. "Now here in this tray . . ."

"Nothing expensive," murmured Sally. Daniel gave her a sharp nudge with his elbow.

Mr. Cohn peered at him. "You work in the mines, eh? And you drive Mr. Guggenheim.

Meshugena—crazy driver. I've seen you. But you're a Jewish boy and this is a Jewish girl and you want to marry her, hah?"

Sally began to laugh. Mr. Cohn sounded as if he were her father. Soon he would be asking Daniel how much money he made. But he seemed to be satisfied. He took out several rings with very small stones. "These I can let you have at a discount. For a fellow from the old country, so to speak. And because your girl is so pretty. And because she comes all the way from Denver."

"I love the one with the pearl, Daniel," Sally exclaimed. "It's so dear!"

Daniel slipped it on her finger.

"It fits! Doesn't need to be sized," said Mr. Cohn.

"Sally Gottesman, I ask you again, will you marry me?"

"Yes, Daniel. I will."

"It's okay," said Mr. Cohn. "You can kiss the girl. I ain't looking."

చ్ఛచ్ఛChapter **12**

"I don't know what to do with you," Dr. Gottesman fumed. "You have always been an unruly child. Sometimes I look at you, a little Jewish girl, and wonder what I did wrong to make you this way. Disobedient. Disrespectful. And now you have come to us with this preposterous story, that you plan to marry that . . . that . . . ragamuffin boy, that miner!"

"It's a very pretty ring," Clara said mildly. "Nothing ostentatious. Not like that ring Nat Wald gave to Lillie, with a diamond so big you could skate on it."

This unfortunate allusion infuriated Dr. Gottesman even more.

"Daniel is not a ragamuffin," Sally insisted. "He

studies hard. He's going to be a doctor, just like you."

"Heh," scoffed her father. "That is what he tells you. What can you believe of a fellow who takes advantage of people's hospitality and sneaks around, seducing an innocent girl!"

To her dismay, Sally was crying now. "Daniel did not seduce me. He is a perfect gentleman. And he didn't sneak around. If anyone sneaked, it was me."

This was not good. Her father turned on her savagely. "Yes, you showed disrespect to your mother and me by sneaking messages to that . . . that miner behind our backs."

"I didn't sneak messages. I just didn't tell you."

"And then you deceived us by going to Leadville with that cock-and-bull story about protecting Frances Jacobs' honor against that whippersnapper rabbi."

Sally tried not to laugh.

"That's disrespectful," said Clara indignantly, "calling the rabbi a whippersnapper."

"But he is. When they hired him I told them I couldn't understand why they couldn't find a grown man, like Rabbi de Sola."

Clara and Sally both gazed at him silently and the doctor calmed down a bit.

"Sally," he said more reasonably. "You know your mother and I love you more than anything on earth. You are our only daughter. But we cannot allow you to ruin your life by marrying a man who doesn't even have the decency to ask for your hand in marriage."

"How could he? He's in Leadville," Sally answered hotly.

Clara feebly joked, "He could telephone." She looked at the recently installed wooden box on the wall with its brass speaker horn. It terrified her.

"There are no telephone lines between Denver and Leadville," said Dr. Gottesman unnecessarily. "There are too many mountains in the way."

"Well," said Clara, briskly getting to her feet. "We'll need to continue this discussion another time. Sally and I are late for a very important meeting of the Non-Partisan Equal Suffrage Organization."

She swept Sally out of the room as the doctor stood there, wondering exactly where the disciplining of his daughter had taken a wrong turn.

"Papa's impossible," Sally fumed as Clara's little two-seater carriage jogged along Colfax Avenue. "He's living in the Middle Ages. The thing that irks him most is that Daniel didn't ask him for my hand like Nat did. Mama, what possessed you to mention Nat Wald?"

"I know. That was very stupid of me. But I just can't abide that little snip Lillie, always showing off. After all, she only got your castoff."

"That's true," Sally agreed with some satisfaction.

"Papa will come around, Sweetie. He loves you. And I believe you. Your Daniel sounds like a splendid young man. I only met him once and he was very polite and well-mannered."

As they approached the new state capitol being constructed on a hill, Sally mused, "I'll bet Otto Mears could figure out a way to put telephone lines over the mountains. He put the roads through the mountains, why not wires?"

"I think he's too busy with the new capitol. I hear he convinced the legislature to put in a dome, like the Capitol in Washington. And all around the dome there will be stained glass windows, each depicting a famous Coloradoan."

"I hope they have a woman," said Sally.

"They'd better," Clara stated firmly as they pulled up in front of the church where the meeting was to be held. Throngs of women were streaming into the building, eager to see the famous Carrie Chapman Catt. It wasn't every day that one of the powerhouse figures of the suffrage movement came to Denver.

Included in the audience were prominent professional women, mainly physicians—Dr. Ethel Strasser of Grand Junction, and Dr. Anna Chamberlain and Dr. Jessie Hartwell of Salida. Journalist Ella Meredith spoke, assuring the women that, "We may fail but there is a very strong chance our enemies may eventually give us our way by default. They will need our votes."

Frances Jacobs spoke in ringing tones of the plight of women who needed to work for a living. "They are occupied with the most menial jobs, working long hours for pay that barely permits them and their children to subsist." On the subject of children, she said, "In our factories, young children of twelve are required to work, depriving them of the necessary healthful fresh air they need to grow into robust adults, cheating them of education." When Frances spoke of the need for education both for women and for deprived youngsters, Sally joined those who stood and cheered.

At last the president of the Equal Suffrage Organization, Martha Pease, introduced Mrs. Carrie Chapman Catt, a chubby woman in her mid-forties from New Rochelle, in New York State.

Mrs. Catt sent greetings from Susan B. Anthony, who had declined to attend the meeting, telling Mrs. Catt that after the defeat the women had suffered when the Colorado State Constitution was written, she didn't have much hope for women's rights in Colorado. But Carrie Chapman Catt did not speak of that. She offered practical advice. "I know many of you are interested in the temperance movement to get rid of the saloons, but Miss Anthony implores you to separate that issue from the all-important one of getting the vote. When we are able to vote, we will elect into office men, and women too, who will dedicate themselves to the social needs which are so important to us.

"I will do what I can to help you. I have a voice like a fog horn and can be heard at out-of-doors meetings. I also have a Sunday school speech—

'The Bible and Woman Suffrage'—which will not offend the most orthodox and has done some good among conservatives."

In the midst of the laughter and cheering, Sally felt a wonderful warmth and strength and happiness. Women did not need to be bossed around and used. They could stand together and help one another.

Clara must have been thinking the same thing, for on the way home she bent over and kissed Sally and said, "Honeybunch, you see, you are not alone. I am on your side and your Aunt Frank is on your side, and so are all your fellow women. It is a sacred right no one can take away from us, to choose the man with whom we are to spend our lives."

Sally couldn't wait to put down the day's excitement on paper, sharing it with Daniel. She soft-pedaled her father's anger, writing:

> Papa has been a little stuffy—you know that old German need for rules. He feels you should have asked for my hand, silly thing. You did ask. You asked me, and that was enough.

Not like Nat Wald, she thought, who went running to Papa and didn't care whether I'd have him or not.

Dr. Gottesman, no doubt under strict orders from his wife, no longer attacked Sally's decision to marry Daniel. He merely regarded her with a pained expression and spoke to her with exaggerated formality.

"If it is not too much trouble, will you pass the salt? . . . How is your nursery school work? Are the children comporting themselves well?"

Sally replied, a bit tartly, that the children did not know how to comport, but they behaved as well as could be expected of five-year-olds.

This went on for some days, and the atmosphere in the house became strained. Clara fluttered. The new maid, Yolanda, a Mexican woman who had replaced Ingrid after she had married Lars and gone to live on their farm, dropped things. Whenever Sally wasn't at the nursery school, she fled to Carrie's to play with Helen, Carrie and Simon's baby daughter.

"Maybe you should take the ring off if it offends your father so much," suggested Carrie.

Sally clutched the ring as if someone were about to tear it from her. "Papa hasn't the faintest idea of what is between Daniel and me. If he killed me, I would not take off the ring," she stormed.

Carrie spooned applesauce into the baby's mouth. "Don't be melodramatic. After all, your father is not a fiend. He's very soft-hearted, and you know it. Everything will be fine."

Several days after this, the family was at breakfast and Dr. Gottesman, as was his habit, was reading aloud tidbits from the Tribune. "150 chickens stolen from a ranch near Golden. Another meeting of the Free Silver club." He growled, "Dr. Cube's Cough Cure, cures consumption. There should be a law! The stuff's nothing but pure alcohol, and the patient gets too drunk to know the difference!"

At that moment, Yolanda brought in the mail. On top of the tray sat an important-looking letter, written on thick creamy stationery. Sally was amazed to see Daniel's familiar scrawl on the envelope addressed to her father.

"Well, what have we here?" said the doctor, slitting open the envelope. He read a few words to himself and then gave Sally a piercing glance and proceeded to read out loud.

> Dear Dr. Gottesman,
> My name is Daniel Rabinowitz and I have the honor (Sally recognized the fine hand of Benjamin Guggenheim) to ask you for your daughter Sarah's hand in marriage. I would have visited you in person, but, as you know, my work keeps me here in Leadville.
> You have met me, but I do not think you know much about me.
> I was born in Berdichev, Russia, twenty years ago and came to the United States with my parents five years ago. Both of my parents have since passed away.
> Berdichev is a city known for Jewish learning. My father was a scholar and a teacher. He taught me not only Talmud and Mishna, but many other subjects that interested him.

In Russia it is not possible for a Jew to attend university. Therefore, because of that and because of the current persecution of our people in Russia, my father decided to come to this country. Before his death, he had arranged to come to Colorado, but we did not do so.

I came to Colorado with my mother, who had consumption. I am very grateful to you for the care you gave her. It is my ambition to also heal those who have this terrible illness. I wish to work in the new Jewish Hospital as a doctor.

In order to do this I must have college credits to go to medical school. My employer, Mr. Benjamin Guggenheim, gave me the books I needed so that I might pass the entrance examination. I am happy to say that I passed and in September will be going to Fort Collins to the agricultural college. I hope to earn enough credits there to go to medical school in Denver.

Sir, I hope this has not bored you, but I wanted you to know that I am a serious person. I will be able to care for your daughter. I love her more than my life. I am sorry that we will have to wait all that time while I finish my studies, but she has agreed to wait for me.

Respectfully,
Daniel Rabinowitz

Dr. Gottesman put down the letter, wiped his glasses with a handkerchief and blew his nose.

Once again, he looked at Sally. "I give my blessing," he said.

She ran to him and threw her arms around his neck. "Thank you, Papa."

With her new teacher's license in hand, Sally applied for a teaching job in the Denver public schools. She was hired to teach first grade; it was felt that her experience teaching young children qualified her well for the job.

A week before school was to open, Miss Abigail West, the principal of the school, called her in for a final interview.

"I see you are wearing an engagement ring," she said severely. "As you know, married women are not permitted to teach. It is felt that if they work outside the home they will neglect their wifely duties." The expression on Miss West's face, as if she had just tasted unexpectedly sour milk, showed what she thought of that rule, which forced her to constantly break in green teachers.

Sally tried her best to look dignified and teacherly, but her thick hair refused to stay in its tight bun and the high collar on her white shirtwaist tickled her neck. "My fiancé is a student," she said primly. "He plans to study medicine. We will not be able to marry for several years."

Miss West smiled more warmly at this information. "Medical school. Like your father Very commendable. It will be a while before you marry."

She nodded approvingly at the circumstance. Then she asked, "What is your feeling about discipline?"

"Children need limits, but fairness," said Sally, thankful that she had been through the fire on this issue already.

Miss West smiled again. "You have had some experience in the nursery school. I trust you will be able to maintain order. Children cannot learn in a chaotic atmosphere." She sighed. With the constant turnover of teachers, this was her biggest headache.

On the first day of school, the children sat in straight rows, their little chairs and desks bolted to the floors. Sally wished she could let them run around and dance and sing the way the children did in nursery school, but first grade was serious business. They sat there, hands folded on their desks, solemn little girls in pinafores, uncomfortably scrubbed little boys.

"Good morning, boys and girls. My name is Miss Gottesman." She started to write her name on the board and then remembered that they couldn't read. Another teacher had advised her, "Never smile until Thanksgiving." but she couldn't help it.

"I hope we will have fun." Fun? The children looked puzzled. Their parents had assured them that fun days were over.

Sally noticed a forked look pass between two boys. "I think Jimmy and Edward would be more comfortable in different seats. Edward, you change with Annette in the first row, and Jimmy with Timothy in the last row." The boys changed seats, looking disgusted. That business about fun didn't mean they would get away with murder. Their older brothers had told them about teachers with eyes in the backs of their heads. This looked like one of those.

The other children, receiving the message from Jimmy and Edward through the special telepathy of childhood, eyed Miss Gottesman warily.

Picking up the rhythm, the atmosphere of a classroom, Sally relaxed. The children knew who was boss.

"Now we'll begin." She turned to the board. "Jimmy, watch me."

Jimmy made a face. It was true. She had eyes in the back of her head.

"This," said Sally. "is the letter A."

It was the eve of Rosh Hashana, and the entire Gottesman family was gathering for dinner before leaving for the temple for the service and the blowing of the shofar. The dining room table was spread with a lace cloth and the porcelain china, and the aroma of honey cake and roast chicken floated in from the kitchen. Carrie, Simon, and baby Helen had arrived, and Carrie was giving numerous instructions to Yolanda, who had raised five children, for the two-hour babysitting stint.

"Si, Señora," nodded Yolanda as the doorbell pealed. Ephraim entered, bringing flowers.

"Where are the Jacobses?" Clara fussed. "We'll be late for temple."

"They'll be here," said Dr. Gottesman. "They're

bringing a guest, I believe."

"You didn't tell me," Clara scolded. "Yolanda, set another place. Who, Sig?

"I don't know. Some forlorn Jew they picked up."

"How like them," Clara sighed. "There they are. I just heard the carriage. Sally, let them in."

But Sally was halfway down the walk by now, yelling.

"I do believe that's young Daniel," said Dr. Gottesman.

"You plotted this, didn't you?" His wife gave him a quick hug.

"You could say that. At least, I sent him the train fare."

"Sorry to be late," Frances explained. "We needed to pick Daniel up at the train."

When they were seated, Dr. Gottesman said the blessing over the bread and broke off pieces of the round New Year challah and distributed them. Then he said, "Daniel, will you say the blessing over the wine?"

Daniel stood up. He had on a new suit and his cheeks were rosy. He seemed embarrassed and Sally noticed that his hand shook a little, but no wine was spilled. Then, in a firm voice, he said the blessing, and added, "*L'shana tovah*, Happy New Year, everyone."

Solemnly, Sally sipped her wine. How could there ever be a happier new year!

ᴡᴡᴡᴡChapter *13*

"What's the matter with her?" asked Daniel. "She shook hands with me as if I had leprosy."

"Miss West feels that her teachers' boyfriends are her personal enemies. There is a rule that teachers must resign if they marry. She considers you a very big threat although I told her it will be years and years before we can marry."

Daniel was staying in Denver until after Yom Kippur and had called for Sally after school. The sky was the impossible blue of October and the air had just a tantalizing hint of coolness, so they decided to walk. Sally had on a neat navy blue suit with leg-o'-mutton sleeves, and Daniel wore his best suit and a cowboy hat and boots acquired in Fort Collins. "Not so many years," he said mysteriously.

Sally stopped. "What? Tell me!"

"Your father has made us an offer. If I come back to Denver to go to medical school, we can get married and live with your parents until we can afford a place of our own."

"Papa said that? That means only . . ."

". . . Three years, if I go to summer school. I must work, too, you know, to pay my board."

She made a little face. "You'll be away during the summer too!"

"I'll be home for holidays. And you can come to Fort Collins during your summer vacation."

"What's it like, Fort Collins?"

He shrugged. "A little *shtetl*, a village. Farms all around, they grow wheat and corn and sugar beets. The students at school are mostly farmers. Good fellows. The people in the town are nice, very friendly."

"Are there any Jewish people?"

"I haven't met any. Sally, watch out for that wagon. The peddler looks half-asleep."

A rickety wagon piled high with old clothes careened around the corner. A bony horse staggered under the listless reins of the haggard-looking, ragged, bearded peddler.

"Simon tells me of something new," remarked Daniel. "They have invented a carriage that can go without horses."

Sally stopped and laughed. "That's silly. How would it be pulled?"

"With an engine. Like a locomotive."

"Well, I would not ride in such a contraption," she tossed her head. "You'd get all dirty from the cinders and coal smoke."

"No. This doesn't run on coal. It has what is called an internal combustion engine. They put gasoline inside and it burns and that sets in motion electricity which makes the carriage go."

"Well," said Sally. "That sounds very dangerous. Why in the world would anyone want such a thing?"

"It goes faster than horses."

"I don't believe it."

"You sound just like your mother, afraid of the telephone. When I get rich I mean to buy me a horseless carriage and I'm going out to the country and drive fast." Daniel's arms made a zooming motion.

"No you won't. It's too dangerous."

"Yes, I will." He looked at her laughing.

Then he stopped short and said "Wait!" and ran into the street. Three tough-looking teenaged boys were throwing stones at the peddler and yelling "Sheeny! Sheeny!"

The peddler had thrown up his hands and was screaming in Yiddish. His horse snorted in alarm.

Daniel darted into the street and grabbed one of the boys and twisted his throwing arm. As the peddler stood up in his wagon, wringing his hands, and Sally looked on in fright, one of the other boys advanced on Daniel and was about to hit him over the head with a stick.

"Look out!" Sally shouted.

Daniel wheeled and kicked the boy in the shins. "I did not," he yelled, "come here all the way from Russia to see this." As the boys retreated, he called after them, "Go home and tell your mama she wants you. And don't you ever harm a peddler again."

The boys ran off and Daniel, followed by Sally, hastened to the peddler. *"Bist du vey geton* . . . are you hurt?"

The peddler was sobbing, tears mixing with blood from a cut on a his cheek. Daniel took out a handkerchief and wiped the man's face while Sally grabbed the bridle and calmed the peddler's horse.

"You'll be all right, Papa," soothed Daniel. "They won't hurt you again."

"Bist du ein doktor?" sobbed the peddler.

"Nein, not yet," said Daniel. "My services are free."

In spite of himself, the peddler smiled. He took hold of the reins. *"Danke,"* he said, and tipped his cap to Sally. *"Danke, maydel."*

Then, looking around fearfully, he flicked the horse's reins and his old horse trotted wearily down the street.

"I need a drink!" said Daniel.

Sally started to turn into a saloon but he grabbed her arm. "Not that kind of drink. Let's find a place where we can get some coffee."

They found a small restaurant and ordered coffee and pastry.

Daniel drank silently, his face grim. Finally, he took some deep breaths and said to her. "You want to know what a pogrom is like? Multiply that a thousand times."

"But these are just ruffians," she said placatingly "Only a few people act like that."

"Throughout history, it was only the ruffians. But they did a lot of damage," he said savagely. "Sometimes I think the Zionists are right, Shayne."

"Who?"

"Some people in Russia. They want to go back to the land, to Palestine. Some of them have already gone."

"That's insane! Palestine is a desert. Everyone knows that. How would they live?"

He leaned forward. "They say they can bring water to the desert. When our ancestors lived there it was a land of milk and honey. If they irrigate it can be so again. Jews will be farmers, the way they used to be. They will own their own land."

"Honey," she said. "I love you for it, but has anyone ever told you that you are a dreamer? Carriages without horses and farms in Palestine!"

In June, 1890, the Jewish Consumptive Relief Society purchased land for the hospital at Jackson and Colfax Avenues, and the fund-raising effort continued. Rabbi Friedman and others on the committee traveled and spoke to groups of Jews throughout Colorado. Money accumulated, little by little, toward the day when construction could begin.

Daniel was able to come to Denver for holidays. Sally renewed old friendships and, with Daniel, once again participated in dances and parties. During the winter holidays they went skating and tobogganing down Capitol Hill, and during spring vacations they picnicked in the foothills.

"But the summer's so long," Sally complained to Carrie, "and Daniel must stay in Fort Collins. He's taking some courses and there's his job at the Linden Hotel."

"What does he do there?" Carrie put little Helen down on the carpet.

"Front desk. He was originally a bellboy, but they promoted him."

"Funny that such a dinky town should have a big hotel."

"Tourists come. It's pretty country, I hear . . . if only I could see it." Sally flounced into a chair, sulking.

Little Helen, holding on to a table leg, slowly got to her feet and started a rocking toddle.

"She's walking!" Carrie shouted.

Startled, the baby sat down with a thump.

"You've scared her." Holding a cookie, Sally crouched in front of Helen. "Baby want cookie? Yum yum." She pretended to bite into it. "Yum, yum."

Helen reached for the cookie.

"Come and get it," enticed Sally, "come to Aunt Sally."

Carrie pulled the laughing baby to her feet and held onto her fingers and then let go. Reaching and squealing, little Helen walked—one step, two steps, three steps—and got a cookie and a large wet kiss in reward.

"I suppose I'll be sorry," Carrie said, grinning. "When they run all over the place you need to watch them every minute."

Sally pulled Helen onto her lap. "I want to have one of these."

"You will," said Carrie comfortably. "So you want to go to Fort Collins."

"What's stopping me is the law, written by Dr. Sigmund Gottesman and his suffragette wife Clara, entitled 'The Impropriety of an Unaccompanied Young Lady Visiting a Young Man.' Carrie, I'll be twenty-one in September!"

Carrie sat, chin in hand, thinking. "The only obstacle is proper chaperonage. Maybe your mother could go."

"We thought of that," said Sally forlornly. "Not much fun for Mama. Besides, she has her activities here. It wouldn't be fair."

"Well," said Carrie. "It seems that the chaperone would need to be at the other end. Doesn't Daniel know some respectable person?"

Evidently, Daniel had been thinking along the same lines. Later that week, a letter arrived saying that he had found a very respectable family, the Howes, who lived near the college and would be willing to rent Sally a room for her visits. "They have a pleasant, large house. Mr. Howe is a pharmacist and Mrs. Howe is president of the women's club at her church."

Sally's parents pondered the suitability of the Howes as chaperones. Sally alternated between nagging them and sulking. At last, it was agreed that the Howe family would save Sally's reputation from irreparable harm.

Daniel met Sally at the Jefferson Street train station and took her for a walk through the town before meeting the Howes. "This is the main street," he said grandly. "College Avenue." The wide unpaved street was crowded with wagons and carriages. All traffic stopped as a parade of cattle, on the way to summer pasture, marched through, leaving mementos behind.

"Colorado gold," said Daniel with agricultural expertise, pointing to a cowpat. "Best thing to spread on your fields."

Sally laughed. "I don't have any fields."

"You don't? Why, Miss Gottesman, what on earth are you doing in Fort Collins? Everybody, at least almost everybody, has fields. Acres and acres. This is Walnut Street. Across the street is my place of business, the Linden Hotel. Come on."

"It's very large," admired Sally, as he guided her

across the dusty street to a three-story brick edifice grandly occupying a corner. It was topped with a stone triangle, defining the corner.

"Best hotel in Northern Colorado. Plate glass door, you'll notice. And a lobby complete with plush draperies." He took her to the ornate check-in desk where a luxuriantly mustached man, wearing a green eyeshade and a striped shirt, said, "Rabinowitz, where have you been?"

"I have the afternoon off, to entertain my fiancée. Sally Gottesman, this is Chip Williams. Sally's come up from Denver."

Chip grasped Sally's hand with a bonebreaking grip. "So this is the sweetie, hey. Well, well."

"I shall entertain Miss Gottesman with a brief refreshment in the lounge," said Daniel.

"Yeah, you do that, kid," said Chip. "But don't forget your shift tomorrow. I can't take care of all the guests by myself."

"This is really elegant," said Sally, looking around the restaurant. "I didn't expect it in Fort Collins. You said it was a . . . a *shtetl.*"

"It is," laughed Daniel. "How about a nice lemonade?"

A waiter appeared, staring boldly at Sally.

"This your girl, Danny?"

"Yes, meet Sally Gottesman. Sally, this is Hank McNeil, a classmate of mine. We'll have the lemonade, and some of that chocolate cake."

"Okay. Please ta meetcha, Sally."

"Danny?" she asked.

"That's my Fort Collins Yankee name."

"And what is your Denver name?"

He thought for a while, with furrowed brow. Then he grinned. "Dr. Rabinowitz. Dr. Daniel Rabinowitz, famous for having the most beautiful wife in all of Denver, in all of North America, in all of the world."

"From your mouth to God's ear," she quoted.

He pressed her hand. "It won't be long, Shayne. Meanwhile, let's have fun in the big city."

While Daniel was working, Mrs. Matilda Howe, a tidy woman in printed cotton who was given to wearing her graying hair in forehead curls, entertained Sally. Creaking back and forth in a wicker rocker on her wide front porch, she recounted in great detail the history of Mr. Howe's family, the descendants of Elijah Howe from Massachusetts, and of her own family, the Osbornes, homesteaders in Nebraska. There was a listing of the family tree, down to second cousins, and a lengthy recital of pioneer hardships from days in the soddy, "when Pa chased a rattlesnake right off my bed," to life on the comfortable family farm. They had settled in Fort Collins because Mr. Howe, who had gone to pharmacy school, felt there were more opportunities in Colorado in the new towns.

"Is there really a fort here?" asked Sally.

"Not any more. They had Camp Collins to chase the Indians, but the Indians left, mostly, and they closed the camp. Now we just have this here cow town."

"It has a good hotel and big houses," said Sally, "for a cow town."

"Well, we have the college, you know. My nephew goes to school with your young man. Your Danny, he has a funny manner of speech. Does he come from a foreign country?"

Sally settled back for the interrogation. Colorado-born, she knew Mrs. Howe would not be satisfied until she knew every shred of information about Sally and Daniel and their respective families. This was not rude nosiness; after all Mrs. Howe had already told her everything about her background, including the story about cousin Wally, who was a bit strange. Sally thought that the Jewish people of Colorado were no different in this respect, except that they already knew everything about one another.

"Daniel was born in Russia."

"That so? We have a whole group of Russians here. Actually, they were Germans who lived in Russia. Confusing. But they are good farmers. Are your fiancé's people of that group?"

"No," said Sally, rocking serenely. "They were just plain Jews running from the pogroms."

Mrs. Howe wrinkled her brow. She had never heard of pogroms.

"Where the Russian soldiers come into a village and kill people and rape the women," Sally said sweetly.

Mrs. Howe flinched at the word rape, hardly used in polite society. She looked at Sally keenly. "Then your fiancé is of the, ah, Hebrew persuasion?"

"Yes," said Sally. "He's also Jewish." Abruptly, she turned her head, stifling a giggle, and pretended to admire the tree-shaded street.

"And yourself. What church do you attend?"

"Temple Emanuel, Denver."

"Ah, then you are also . . ."

"Of the Hebrew persuasion."

Mrs. Howe settled back, regarding Sally, and creaked her rocker a few times. "You are quite fair in complexion, and your hair is blonde." This was said in a mildly accusing tone, as if Sally didn't really have the right to have blonde hair, since she was Jewish.

"Many Germans are blonde. My family came from Germany originally."

"That's so. The Russian Germans. Some of them are blonde." She creaked thoughtfully. "In the town where I came from we had a Jewish family. Levy. Fine people. They owned a clothing store. Does your father own a store?"

"No, he's a doctor."

Mrs. Howe was quite astounded to hear this.

"Many Jews are doctors," said Sally. "The famous Jewish philosopher Maimonides was a doctor."

"Maimonides. Does he live in Denver?"

"No, he lived in Toledo."

"Oh," said Mrs. Howe with a satisfied air. "Ohio."

"Twelfth century," remarked Sally, studying the large hydrangea bush below the porch railing.

"Oh," said Mrs. Howe, momentarily stumped. "That was before Columbus . . ."

Sally wanted to add, "also before Ohio," but refrained.

Finally Mrs. Howes said triumphantly, "It must have been the other Toledo."

"Right. Spain."

"Toledo, Spain. I've heard of that," said Mrs. Howe gravely. "Well, Mr. Howe and I belong to Assembly of God church. We set great store by the Old Testament and the Hebrews in the Bible."

Sally smiled, pleased that Mrs. Howe recognized the worth of the Hebrew Bible. "Maybe it was Cordoba, Spain," she reflected aloud.

"Would you and your young man care to come to our strawberry social next Sunday?"

"We'd like that very much. Thank you." Sally relaxed. The interview was over and she had passed.

"Strawberry social! I wanted to take some horses and go up Horsetooth Mountain," Daniel complained that evening.

"We are going to the strawberry social," said Sally firmly. "If not, you can forget about the Howes arrangement."

The social, with home-made strawberry ice cream and strawberry shortcake and cowboy music, proved to be enjoyable.

But one thing puzzled Daniel. "What are they whispering about?"

"Mrs. Howe is pointing us out. We're her prize exotic specimens, real Israelites of the Hebrew persuasion."

The next day Daniel took Sally on horseback up a wagon trail called the Masonville Road to the mountain called Horsetooth because of its pointed peak that looked exactly like a horse's tooth. They rode slowly up the steep trail and then sat on a ledge overlooking the blue hills of the Front Range.

The following day they picnicked on the bank of the river called Cache le Poudre. "Hide the powder," said Sally. "What a strange name."

"Not at all," Daniel explained. "The French trappers hid their stores of gunpowder near the river."

And so the months passed. Holidays in Denver and long summer days in Fort Collins. There was teaching. And working on the hospital committee.

Then, amazingly, it was 1892. As the orchestra played "Auld Lang Syne," at the New Year's Eve party at Temple Emanuel, Sally and Daniel embraced. It would be a wonderful year, the year Daniel would graduate and enter medical school and the year they would marry. And finally, construction of the Jewish Consumptive Hospital would commence.

Chapter 14

In May Daniel graduated from the Colorado State Agricultural College. Sally and her parents journeyed to Fort Collins for the occasion and stayed at the Linden Hotel. Bashfully, Daniel endured the kisses and handshakes. Seeing him so excited and happy, Sally was deeply thankful that, like the other graduates, he was surrounded by loving relatives.

"There's a rumor among my colleagues in Denver," said Dr. Gottesman to Daniel, "that your grade on the qualifying examination for Gross Medical College was one of the highest they ever recorded."

"Well, you did coach me," Daniel grinned. "And in aggie school, you learn a lot doctoring horses and cows."

Two weeks later, Sally and Daniel were married at Temple Emanuel under a canopy, called a *chuppa*, fragrant with lilacs. Simon was best man and Carrie, in yellow organdy, was matron of honor. Little Helen was the flower girl. Doll-like in white ruffles, she toddled down the aisle, spilling flowers in every direction. Years later, Rabbi Friedman recalled two things about the wedding. First, when Daniel broke the glass, the rabbi worried that the temple would have to install a new floor. Second, at the end of the ceremony, "The five most unnecessary words I've ever spoken were 'You may kiss the bride.'"

It was a lovely June day. Even the usual five o'clock rain held off as Sally's old confirmation class friends mixed at the outdoor reception with the teachers from her school. Lars and Ingrid had driven in from their farm and a platoon of husky Aggie students from Fort Collins made a beeline for Sally's young teachers, as Miss West looked on in alarm. But there was little harm done, except that a third-grade teacher became enamored of a young wheat farmer from Weld County.

Miss West, looking grim in a high-collared blue suit, said grudgingly, as she kissed Sally, "You were one of our best teachers." She fixed an accusing eye on Daniel and said icily, "Congratulations."

"I'm going to continue teaching," Sally told her. "The nursery school doesn't have that rule about married teachers."

"Yes, ah yes." Miss West regarded Daniel venomously. "And your, er, husband. Is he still planning to be a doctor?"

"He's been accepted in the Gross Medical School," said Sally. "Right now he's working at Appel's department store."

Miss West examined Daniel with a slightly warmer expression. "Well, I hope you'll do half as well as your father-in-law, young man. Dr. Gottesman is very well regarded in Denver."

"She likes us," Sally remarked as the principal swept off toward the punch.

"Is that why she gave us that ugly bronze statue of Atlas holding up the world? How soon can we get out of here?"

"Soon. I need to throw my bouquet."

The third-grade teacher caught the bouquet and Sally and Daniel left in a hired carriage for the train station and a week in Colorado Springs.

When Sally and Daniel returned from their honeymoon, they settled into the little apartment made by combining Sally's and Simon's old rooms.

The summer disappeared in a whirl of good times and work.

Daniel clerked in Appel's store to pay their way, but during his scarce time off there were picnics at Eagle Rock and free concerts at the new Elitch Gardens, often with other young couples. Among them were Nat and Lillie Wald. Nat regarded Daniel with the expression of an elk who has lost an antler-tangling fight, and Lillie showed off her rings and, knowing that Daniel and Sally were still living with Sally's parents, bragged about her house and servants.

"The Walds are obnoxious," said Daniel, using one of his favorite new English words.

"I know," sighed Sally, "but they come with the territory."

It was an exciting day when the hospital committee assembled in the Gottesmans' dining room to go over final plans with the architect. Sally sat quietly in the background, listening.

"We need windows, lots of windows," declared Frances Jacobs, "to let in sunshine and air. And porches where the patients can sleep in the open air during the good weather."

As the committee members pored over his drawings, the architect explained details of the exterior. The hospital was to be an elegant structure of red brick with a white stone trim. The front entrance would be imposing, the doorway beneath a tower with a steep, pointed roof.

A short time later, the workmen commenced digging the foundation for the building. Sally was present as several reporters clustered around, asking questions of the committee members who were watching the operation. "How many patients do you expect to accommodate?" inquired a reporter from the Rocky Mountain News.

"We hope to treat sixty-five patients," replied Dr. Gottesman. "They may stay free of charge for six months. Patients can come from any place in the United States. The only provision is that someone responsible guarantee that they will not become a burden on Denver charity. We're sorry, but we don't want to attract people who will remain public charges. Denver has already had more that its share of that."

"We understand that this is a Jewish hospital," said the reporter. "Does that mean that the hospital is only for Jewish patients?"

"Definitely not," said Frances Jacobs. "The hospital is a gift from the Jewish people of Colorado to tuberculosis sufferers, whatever their background."

Whenever they could, Sally and Daniel visited the site where the hospital was slowly taking shape. Each day new walls appeared, brickwork covered the exterior and shining windows were set in place on all sides of the building. The front tower went up inside a nest of wooden scaffolding and workers swarmed over the roof, nailing down shingles. As the work inside progressed, the airy large rooms took shape: patients' sleeping quarters, recreation rooms, and a huge kitchen where nourishing meals would be prepared. In September a lawn was planted and bushes placed around the building. As the building stood gleaming in its newness, the only thing missing was the cornerstone to fill the gap left by the masons.

At last the dreamed-of day arrived—the official placing of the cornerstone on October 9, 1892. People flocked to the ceremonies from all parts of the city. The roads were jammed with carriages and the cable car trolleys and new electric trolleys, which had replaced the horsecars, were packed.

Rabbi Friedman, who had grown a mustache and looked dignified enough even for Dr. Gottesman's satisfaction, spoke first. "As pain knows no creed, so is this building the prototype of the grand idea of Judaism, which casts aside no stranger, no matter of what race or blood." He was followed by clergymen of the various churches, the mayor, and various dignitaries.

Beaming on the platform, Frances Jacobs held onto her big hat against a strong breeze. When she rose to speak, she had a fit of coughing and shivered a little. Her voice was hoarse as she detailed the plight of those she knew so well, the penniless sick who fell, often hemorrhaging, in the streets. "We will care for them tenderly, and make them well," she said.

Sally watched Frances worriedly. Dr. Gottesman said, "I don't like that cold. Remind me, Clara, to give her a tonic. She's been working entirely too hard."

In November the weather turned harsh. The wind brought gritty snow. "Pneumonia weather," said Dr. Gottesman ominously.

The new telephone rang constantly and the doctor was busy visiting patients at all hours. When he could take time off from his studies, Daniel drove the buggy to relieve the doctor.

"I'm worried about Frances, Sig," Clara said one evening after dinner. "Her cold gets no better."

"She must stay home. I have told her many times to do so," Dr. Gottesman replied wearily.

On November 13, after a rainy week, with the wind howling outside, the family had gathered for a peaceful evening in front of the fire. Barney, the dog, now full of years and loving his sleep, snoozed at Dr. Gottesman's feet. In a corner, Daniel pored over a medical book. Clara tended to some sewing, and Sally was deep in a new romantic novel. A cylinder on their newest acquisition, the phonograph invented by Mr. Edison, wheezed out a violin sonata.

The telephone pealed. "Mercy!" Clara jumped. The sound still startled her.

Sighing and shaking his head, the doctor went into the hall to answer it. It would be for him. It usually was for him.

"I see," he said, becoming tight-lipped. "Well, there no sense going over what she did. I told her to stay home. I'll be right there."

He turned to his family. At the sight of the expression on his face, Sally began to tremble.

"Frances has taken a turn for the worse. It looks like pneumonia."

He started for the door, followed by the rest of

the family.

"She was getting better," Uncle Abraham wailed when they arrived. "Then she got a message that one of those families she cares for was in need. 'Frankie,' I said, 'Let someone else go.' 'There are children,' she said, 'and they have no coal. No heat, Abraham, in this miserable weather.' And off she went, in the rain. I should have held her down by force."

The Jacobs children, Evelyn and Benjamin, arrived late that night. Then Rabbi Friedman came. There were no medicines to fight pneumonia, only the patient's own strength. As the disease progressed, it reached a climax. Then, if all was well, the fever subsided and the patient recovered. If not, the patient died.

Clara and Sally silently served tea and tried to get the others to eat something. The atmosphere grew thick with tension as they waited out the crisis through the night.

Abraham remained in the sick room with the doctor and Rabbi Friedman stayed downstairs, trying, without words, to offer comfort.

Suddenly Dr. Gottesman appeared at the head of the stairs and beckoned to the rabbi, who hurried up to the sick room.

"What does this mean?" Evelyn got to her feet, distraught.

"It will be all right," said Clara, tight-lipped.

But it was not all right. The doctor came down

the stairs, opened his hands and said bleakly, "She's gone," and burst into tears.

Sally wanted to scream. But Clara caught her hand. "We're the comforters," she murmured. They did their best, but the family was inconsolable. "She was only forty-nine," Abraham kept saying, rocking back and forth. "Why did I let her go out? It's my fault."

"No, Papa," said Evelyn. "Mama had to help. She gave every moment of her life."

Finally Dr. Gottesman told Daniel, "The rabbi will bring me home. Please, take the ladies home. There's nothing more they can do now."

For once, his head bowed, Daniel drove slowly. He was praying quietly in Hebrew. In the back seat, Clara wept. "It was not necessary. Who will help the poor people now? What of Abraham? What will become of him? She was his life."

Sally could not talk. She could only lean against Daniel as he put one arm about her and kept on praying.

Two thousand people thronged Temple Emanuel for the funeral of Frances Jacobs. Nine organizations and all departments of the city and state governments were represented, and eulogies were delivered by Rabbi Friedman and three Christian clergymen. The Charity Organization Society, which Frances Jacobs had founded and which later became the Community Chest, published a memorial statement in the Rocky Mountain News.

Sally, seated with the mourners, remembered Frances' words: "How are you to have that sympathy for the poor, miserable creatures whom you meet? It is only by having a oneness with man and God."

Otto Mears, friend of Frances Jacobs and builder of roads, consulted with the committee building the new state capitol. There were to be sixteen panels, holding stained-glass portraits of significant Coloradoans. And representing the women of Colorado would be Frances Jacobs, "Mother of Charities." Her face would remind visitors to the golden dome of the many valorous women who had helped to form the state. It would also be a message from the Jewish people of Denver that the meaning of their ancient Covenant was understood—to care for all within the family of man.

Jacob Appel, who had worked with Frances Jacobs in the Associated Charities, suggested naming the new hospital, The Frances Jacobs Memorial Hospital, and the Jewish Consumptive Relief Society members agreed.

Several months after Frances' death, Sally and Daniel were standing in front of the new hospital when the placard was fixed above the entrance: The Frances Jacobs Hospital.

Daniel turned to Sally. "You see, Shayne, the work goes on." He rubbed his hands and his face had that same eagerness it had when, driving

Benjamin Guggenheim's carriage, he galloped the horses down the hill.

She took his hands in hers. "You should wear your gloves. It's cold." But before he put on his gloves, she took off her own and pressed her hands against his. As Ingrid had said, they were the same: two index fingers, mirrors of each other, one longer than the other, but both slender and tapering, with square nails.

Sally saw something else in Daniel's hands. These were the hands that would soothe those in pain, that would know exactly how to heal. Slowly and solemnly, she kissed each of his palms, giving them her blessing.

Afterword

Daniel was not to get his wish to work in the hospital until 1899, when he and Sally were living in their own house with their two little girls. Upon graduation from medical school, he entered his father-in-law's practice until the time, much delayed, when the hospital would open.

The reason for the delay was a devastating economic depression that hit Colorado in 1893. The federal government decided to replace silver with gold to back its currency. In a generally weak economy, this decision was fatal to Colorado silver mines. Thousands of workers lost their jobs, and those who earned their living supplying these people suffered severe deprivation.

With the spiraling of economic failures, there

was no money available to equip and staff the hospital. The Jewish community simply could not afford it.

Funds previously had been collected only from Colorado Jews, but it was now evident that an appeal needed to go out to Jewish communities in the rest of the country. After all, sufferers from tuberculosis were not only a Colorado problem; they came from all over the nation. The B'nai B'rith lodge contacted other lodges throughout the country. Rabbi Friedman, along with David May of Leadville, journeyed throughout the Eastern states telling the story of the hospital and soliciting funds.

Finally, in November, 1899, the hospital, re-named the "National Jewish Hospital for Consumptives," opened its doors. As the sign, "The Frances Jacobs Hospital" was taken down and a placard with the new name was installed, the mayor of Denver spoke:

This consummates the work begun years ago by one of Denver's noble pioneer women, Mrs. Frances Jacobs, but on a broader and more extended scale than she had planned. While "The Frances Jacobs Hospital" will not exist in name, it will be a pleasure to know that out of her efforts has grown an institution, national in its scope, and dedicated to the humane and charitable work in which during her lifetime she so earnestly engaged."

For many years, the hospital treated tuberculosis

patients in the only way available, offering them clean beds, nourishing food, rest and light exercise, and plenty of fresh Colorado air. A special wing, called the Preventorium, cared for sickly children in danger of contracting tuberculosis, providing them with healthy nourishment and a clean, airy environment. Another service of the hospital was a Children's Shelter, which took care of the children of patients.

As antibiotics lessened the scourge of tuberculosis, the hospital served other needs, most notably the treatment of asthma. Children with severe asthma came from all over the nation to benefit from the climate and the latest medical techniques, for the National Jewish Hospital, no longer a single building, had become world-renowned.

Increasingly, prominent physicians came to the hospital to participate in advanced research. Renamed in 1985 the National Jewish Center for Immunology and Respiratory Medicine, the hospital has become a center for research on the nature of the T-cell receptor gene, an important immune system element.

Sadly, there has been a renewal of a vicious strain of tuberculosis, resistant to antibiotics, particularly striking AIDS patients. The scientists at the National Jewish Center are hard at work looking for new medicines that will defeat their old enemy.

Glossary

Ark Enclosure where the Torah is kept in the synagogue

Bima Altar in the synagogue

bucher (Yiddish) male student

challah Braided loaf of bread used on the Sabbath and for other ceremonial occasions

Chanukah (Also spelled Hanukkah) holiday celebrating the victory of the Jews over Antiochus and the purifying of the Temple, especially the miracle when a tiny portion of sacred oil lasted for eight days; marked by eating *latkes*, gift-giving, lighting the *menorah*, and playing a game with a top called a *dreidel*

feisele (Yiddish) little feet

grogger Noisemaker. When the Book of Esther is read at Purim, at every mention of Haman's name, children twirl their groggers and boo loudly (Purim is not a "dignified" holiday!)

Haman In the Book of Esther, the greedy Persian prime minister concocted lies against the Jews so that he could kill them and confiscate their property, but Queen Esther told the king of the plot, and Haman was hanged instead. This rescue of the Jews is celebrated on the holiday of Purim

hamantaschen A three-cornered, filled pastry, eaten on Purim to symbolize Haman's hat

Hasidim (also **Chassidim**) Members of an Orthodox Jewish group, begun 200 years ago to restore joy to worship with singing and dancing.

Kabbala Mystical Jewish writings

Kaddish Prayer of praise. A special Kaddish is said to memorialize the dead

kinder (Yiddish) children

kosher Proper, fit. Kosher foods are prepared in a certain way, according to Jewish law. Animals are slaughtered in a manner designed to give the least pain and to drain all blood. Certain foods, especially pig products and shellfish, are forbidden, or unkosher

latke (Yiddish) potato pancake

menorah Branched candlestick

meshugena (Yiddish) crazy person

minyan Ten Jews over the age of thirteen, necessary for a worship service

Mishna   Commentary on the Bible

mitzvah   (Hebrew) Commandment; commonly translated as good dead

Mogen David   Star of David

neshama   (Hebrew) soul

Purim   Festive spring holiday, celebrated with masquerade parties and giving of small gifts. Named for the casting of lots, called *pur*, to establish the order in which Haman would hang the Jews

Reform Judaism   Liberalizing movement in Judaism, dating from mid-nineteenth century in Germany. Most worship is done in the native language (English in the U.S.) rather than in Hebrew. Emphasis is on education and social justice. In addition to Bar Mitzvah and Bat Mitzvah, sixteen-year-olds are confirmed after additional education

Rosh Hashanah   Jewish New Year, occurring in the fall

seder   Festive meal, eaten at Passover, during which the story of the Exodus from Egypt is recounted

Shabbos   Yiddish for Sabbath; Hebrew is *Shabbat*

Shavuot   Spring holiday, celebrating the harvesting of the First Fruits as well as the giving of the Ten Commandments. Often used to mark confirmation of sixteen-year-olds

sheitel   Wig worn after marriage by some Orthodox Jewish women in order not to be attractive to men other than their husbands

shayne maydel   (Yiddish) beautiful girl

shofar   Ram's horn, blown to announce the New Year or other important occasion

shtetl   (Yiddish) small village

shul   (Yiddish) study house; small orthodox synagogue

Talmud   Commentary on the Mishnah, with many stories and legal interpretations

Torah   The Hebrew Bible, also known as the Five Books of Moses. Printed in book form or written by hand on a parchment scroll and kept in the Ark in the synagogue

tzedakah   Obligation to help those less fortunate, from the Hebrew word meaning "justice"

Yom Kippur   Day of Atonement, a fast day when worshipers atone for their failings and ask forgiveness